YOUR BUSINESS YOUR WEALTH

CORY SHEPHERD

PAUL ADAMS

ISBN 978-0-9986446-0-8

Contents

To Jeff Miller:
Thank you for serving as our primary reader—
the fingerprints of your expertise and insight
are all over this book!

Introduction

H OW MANY BUSINESS OWNERS DO YOU KNOW? IF YOU'RE AN ENTRE-
preneur like us, you can probably find 100 or more just by scrolling
through your LinkedIn page and other social media.

Next question: How many business owners do you know who have the
kind of freedom that would allow them to travel for a year? Or take a six-
month sabbatical from work? Probably not many.

Now for the kicker: How many business owners do you know who
have sold their businesses and have been retired for a decade or more? The
retired business owner who simply gets "mailbox money" to support their
lifestyle is like a baby pigeon: everyone believes they exist, though most
people have never seen one.

As managers of a successful financial strategy and investment planning group aimed specifically at entrepreneurs, we can tell you unequiv-
ocally that they are real. Over the years, we've helped countless business
owners retire with more than enough for their families to be both secure
and happy. With this book, you could be one of them.

How to Read This Book

THIS BOOK MAY HAVE COME INTO YOUR POSSESSION A NUMBER OF DIF-ferent ways. You may have seen us speak at a conference, liked what you heard, and wanted to learn more. Perhaps the title grabbed your attention at the bookstore because of where you're currently at in life. Perhaps a big online retailer suggested it based on other books you've viewed or purchased. There's also a good chance that this book was put in your hands by your CPA, business partner, or a fellow member of a mastermind group—someone who knows you well enough to understand how this book can help you get to where you want to go.

We know that so many people are coming to this book from so many different paths, which is why we wrote it to be as easy to reference as possible. So while it can certainly be read from end to end, you may also choose to jump ahead to a topic that is particularly relevant to an issue you are dealing with in this moment. To help you decide where to begin, here's a breakdown of the book's three main parts.

Part 1: Avoid the Entrepreneur's Trap (Chapters 1–2)

Business owners regularly overestimate the value of their businesses. This costly mistake tranquilizes them into non-action regarding their personal finances. It derails any chance they have of building long-term, impenetrable financial security. While it's only natural for a business owner to take pride in what they've built, the mistake comes when business owners assume others share their beliefs about how much their business is worth. Furthermore, the amount someone is willing to pay for it is much different than the amount of income you can expect to earn from it in the years to come. That is a vital distinction you must make to avoid the worst-case scenario so many owners find themselves in. After reading this section, you'll be able to see your business through clearer eyes and will understand why owning and selling a business will not be enough for most people to provide financial security for the rest of their lives, and what you can start doing about it right away.

Part 2: Plan Ahead to Ensure You Have Enough (Chapters 3–6)

What does it mean to build your personal balance sheet so you're prepared for long-term financial success? What does it take to do it? How can your business and personal balance sheets work *together* to build that long-term financial success? Most people assume it's an either/or proposition. This is another costly mistake that this section will ensure you avoid. Once you understand that your personal balance sheet and business balance sheet are different, you'll be on the path to building the financial future of your dreams (whatever they may be).

Part 3: Make the Most out of the Business You've Built (Chapters 7–10)

A wealth of information exists about how to improve your finances, whether from attorneys, CPAs, or all the business journals available to professional advisors. Unfortunately, the vast majority of this information isn't written for business owners and the unique challenges they need to address. And the experts who do address business owners are either trying to sell a specific product or focus on helping owners grow their businesses rather than grow out of their businesses. In this final part of the book, we're going to "translate" the vital information you need so it's easy to digest and understand how to make your business successful in the long run, achieve long-term engagement from your employees, and avoid mistakes that are all too common among investors (hint: one of them is mutual funds).

So, if you're dealing with a particular problem at the moment and you see which section will help the most, by all means, jump ahead. However, we also hope you'll find time to read the book from start to finish, as the way we explain certain concepts spans several chapters. We promise you it will be worthwhile to go through all of this information.

Thank You, Reader

Before we proceed, we want to take a moment to thank you for reading this book. It is an honor to share our insights with a like-minded business-person. We truly hope it will change your life.

Also, if you do find it helpful, please share it with your business partner or professional advisory team. We want to make sure that as many people as possible can benefit from the lessons learned during our professional journeys.

PART 1:
AVOID THE ENTREPRENEUR'S TRAP

Chapter 1:
Your Business Is Amazing—
and It's Not Enough

T HE TITLE FOR THIS CHAPTER ISN'T A PERSONAL JAB. (HOW COULD IT be? We don't even know you.) For most business owners, though, it is an accurate statement.

As entrepreneurs and business owners ourselves, we know what it takes to start a business and the feeling of pride when it is successful. We started Sound Financial Group to educate our clients about how to keep more of the money they earn, and it's grown beyond our wildest dreams. But we also know that selling the company one day will not be enough, by itself, to ensure we are able to provide for our families for the rest of our lives.

In this chapter, we're going to dig into why your business is not enough. We are also going to explain why so many entrepreneurs miss this—and what it costs them in the long term.

Entrepreneurs Are the Exception

Did you know that only about 6% to 14% of the world's population are entrepreneurs? The larger number is probably a bit skewed, too. That statistic comes from the Global Entrepreneurship Measure and includes people who are currently at a job but considering entrepreneurship, not just those who already own their own businesses. In any case, we entrepreneurs are a very small part of the population, despite the fact that companies that employ fewer than 500 people account for 95% of all businesses.

Think about that for a moment. The majority of *all* businesses are owned by entrepreneurs. As individuals our numbers are small, but as business owners our impact is absolutely massive. We drive innovation, bring new products and services to market, and employ tens of millions across the country.

However large our impact, the fact is, successful entrepreneurial ventures are the exception, not the rule. If you followed every company that gets started this year, only about 20% to 30% of them will survive a decade. Keep in mind, too, that "survive" just means the business is operational and filed a tax return. It doesn't say anything about whether the company is actually successful. If you used a different metric—say, the threshold a company has to hit in order to join an organization like the Entrepreneurs' Organization, which is more than $1 million in revenue—that 20% to 30% number plummets.

Here's another way to look at it. Back in 2014, Paul Adams spoke to a group of Seattle Entrepreneurs' Organization members. There were about 35 of them gathered around the stage, and it dawned on him that, given the 20% to 30% survival rate statistics, roughly 175 people had to have started businesses a decade earlier in order for that group of entrepreneurs to still own a business today. It gets worse (or better, depending on your side of the curve) if you think bigger: all the businesses in that room generated over $1 million of revenues per year, meaning *3,500* businesses had to have started, to arrive at this small group of high-performing survivors 10 years later.

As a successful entrepreneur, you are a rare breed. But most of us don't see ourselves that way. For one thing, you're probably not focused on other people's success—or lack thereof. You're focused on your business and making sure it continues to grow. That focus is probably one of the reasons your business is still in operation. At the same time, when you do look around at your peers, the entrepreneurs who didn't make it aren't there. You're only seeing the success stories. The failed businesses disappear, replaced by the ones that make it.

Don't forget that you're the exception, and as such you have unique challenges to deal with that the rest of the population never has to think about. As we'll delve into shortly, your financial future depends on recognizing that entrepreneurs need to plan differently than everyone else does.

High Financial Rewards Don't Translate into Long-Term Financial Security

As you are probably aware, one of the biggest benefits of being a business owner is that you have the potential for an unlimited income. There's no one above you to say, "This is how much you'll make this year" or "Here's how much we can afford to pay you." You could, quite literally, earn as much as you want.

Sure, increasing your income demands increased work, but at the end of the day it's up to you how much you put in and how much you take out of your business. Most people who work for someone else can't imagine what that's like. It's an amazing feeling. Maybe you've experienced it firsthand, too. You realized you wanted to buy a new home—even a second home. Maybe you just wanted to add more to your child's college fund, or you have set your eyes on a new boat.

It is this key upside of being an entrepreneur that can blind us to the truth about what our financial planning requires. Though it may feel this way sometimes, your income is *not actually unlimited*! Your income potential over the life of your business is higher than most others, but it is not infinite. For perspective, picture a giant bucket sitting next to the front door of your headquarters, containing all the revenue your business will earn over your lifetime. You don't know exactly how large the bucket would need to be, though in some cases it would be a very large bucket indeed. Nonetheless, it is not infinite.

We don't bring this up to break your spirit, but to help you realize the opportunity. Most people who sell products and services to your business want you to think of that income as unlimited so you are more freewheeling with the business checkbook. We may be the lone voice in your world urging you to understand and own the finite nature of your resources. This is because anything that is valuable must also be scarce. If every decision to deploy capital is made with that large-but-not-endless bucket image in the back of your mind, think how much more strategic you might be with your long-term growth planning and daily spending decisions.

Of course, there are plenty of other perks besides *near*-infinite income potential. For example, when you go on vacation, you may take the opportunity to scope out real estate that could be used to expand your business. As a result, you get to write off part of your trip as a tax deduction. If you go to a business conference, you can bring your family to spend time together. You can make a mini-vacation out of it while still enjoying the write-off you're entitled to for the business expense involved.

Most entrepreneurs wisely use their businesses to purchase their vehicles, too.

The list goes on and on, but all of these benefits of being an entrepreneur—including the high levels of income we're able to achieve—don't automatically translate into sufficient amounts of money for funding the rest of your life.

This is why it is incredibly important for your future that you understand how your *personal balance sheet* differs from that of anyone who doesn't own their own business.

Understanding Your Personal Balance Sheet

When we say, "personal balance sheet," we are referring to your personal finances—not your business's finances. We continually remind clients, "You build financial independence on your personal balance sheet, not your business balance sheet." We will even take it a step further: you will never have the independence or autonomy you first desired when going into business, solely on the strength of your business balance sheet. Your business exists, and has always existed, for two reasons. One is to make real the specific kind of impact or change in the world that you were meant to make. The other is as a tool to create the cash flow you require for all your other needs, wants, and goals. All autonomy and freedom to "Design and Build a Good Life" (a phrase you will hear more about from us) will stem from personal cash flow and personal balance sheet management.

The Entrepreneur's Trap

Imagine for a moment your life in a very different situation: instead of owning your company, you are an executive at a large corporation. You get a regular paycheck, and you have a 401(k). If you're a high-level executive you might own company stock, but you understand you're not going to see a huge payout if the company is sold.

No one in that position thinks for a moment that the company they work for will provide the cash flow they need for the rest of their life. When a successful executive working for a big company doesn't save for retirement—year after year—other people find that irresponsible. They warn them to get their act together and remind them that, someday, they won't be getting that regular paycheck.

Unfortunately, this is often not the case for entrepreneurs. While we have our own perks like tax write-offs, we don't have company-funded retirement plans. Even worse, our culture applauds the entrepreneur who reinvests every single dollar they have back into their business. "Good for you, keep believing in yourself," they say, as they celebrate the ideal of the solitary, self-made American hero taking on the world.

We urge you to celebrate your success in a different way. Recognize that after a certain stage in your business, "Putting money back into the business" is code for "Not diversifying my investments and not harvesting any of my business's incredible growth for my family's future."

As entrepreneurs, we have a much different relationship with our businesses than someone who works for a company, and that relationship changes over time:

- **Phase 1: Working a Job**—At the very beginning, you owned your business, but you also did every (or, at least, almost every) job required to keep it in operation. You wore every hat and your business card was just your name followed by a long list of titles and roles. You were Employee of the Month, every month. So, while you were the business owner, it felt like you were just as much an employee, too.
- **Phase 2: Building a Business**—After you experienced enough business growth, a major shift occurred. Instead of working *in* your

business, you could finally begin working *on* your business. This meant looking at the systems, structures, and training required to keep your business growing. That said, while you were able to back off a bit from the day-to-day tasks, you weren't in the clear yet. You were working on your business, but you still spent plenty of time wearing a couple of other hats to ensure things ran smoothly.

- **Phase 3: Running the Business**—Finally, you were able to put all those other hats away and simply run your business. Now, you're working on your business full time. Your business card has just one title, and you're handing out Employee of the Month plaques to actual employees.

The other great thing about phase 3 of the business owner's evolution is that your company now becomes an attractive opportunity for others: it becomes *sellable.* During those first two phases, that's not the case. No one wants to buy a company in that first phase, because they'd really just be buying a job. Phase 2 isn't ideal, either. People buy businesses because they want to be full-time business owners, not business builders. No one wants to *buy* a job. People want to buy during phase 3 when the company is fully up and running.

For the vast majority of entrepreneurs, phase 3 is the goal. It's the pinnacle. Conventional wisdom says that once you've made it to phase 3, you've made it. You've started the company. You've made it successful. Most importantly, you now have your nest egg in place. When you're finally ready to retire, you can just sell your company for enough to fund your entire retirement. You're set for life.

Except you're not.

This is an entrepreneur's trap, and it's a costly one. Imagine working hard your entire life and coming to retirement only to find that you're going to have to live off just a *small* fraction of what you used to make when you were working full time. How would you feel about that? What kinds of sacrifices would you need to make? Would you look back and wonder if it was all worth the effort?

Fortunately, this fate is avoidable. You can enjoy your passion for entrepreneurship without viewing your business as an anchor that's keeping you from the joys of retirement. However, the only way to achieve this is by making a key distinction, one that occurs during the fourth phase of owning a business—one which far too many business owners never reach.

This final stage is when you realize that your personal balance sheet and your business's balance sheet are not the same. You begin moving a significant portion of the wealth generated by your business to your personal balance sheet to be invested in your own financial security.

Early on you devoted all of your resources to supporting your business, and now your business starts to return the favor, becoming one of the main supporting assets on your personal balance sheet. You are also discovering other investments and assets that will provide you with the income you need to continue living the life you want long after you've sold your business. When you are able to view your business as one of the many assets feeding your personal balance sheet, you take a massive step away from the entrepreneur's trap. We call this the "design stage." (More on this in chapter 4.)

An All-Too-Common Example of the Entrepreneur's Trap

Before we go any further, we want to make sure that you understand how easy it is to fall into the entrepreneur's trap.

For example, let's say that you currently make $400,000 a year as a business owner. That's your taxable income. It's the amount you've grown accustomed to—the amount you use to fund your lifestyle. Of course, you have other perks, as we covered earlier—such as the ability to purchase cars through your business and write off certain trips—but for the sake of this example, let's just stay focused on your annual income of $400,000.

Once you retire, it makes sense that you want to keep a comparable lifestyle, which means you would still need another $400,000 available to you every single year. How much in assets do you need to create that same amount of income once you leave your business?

A starting point in answering that question is "the 4% rule," which establishes the maximum withdrawal rate from your assets in retirement. This rate has become the rule of thumb for most financial advisors when it comes to initial withdrawals during retirement. A famous financial planner named William Bengen quantified this rate in 1994. After testing numerous withdrawal rates and applying historical returns for stocks and bonds, he concluded that 4% was the optimal amount for those who wanted their savings to last at least 30 years.[1]

At a distribution rate of 4%, you would need $10 million to draw from in order to see the $400,000 every year that you must have to fund your lifestyle throughout retirement.

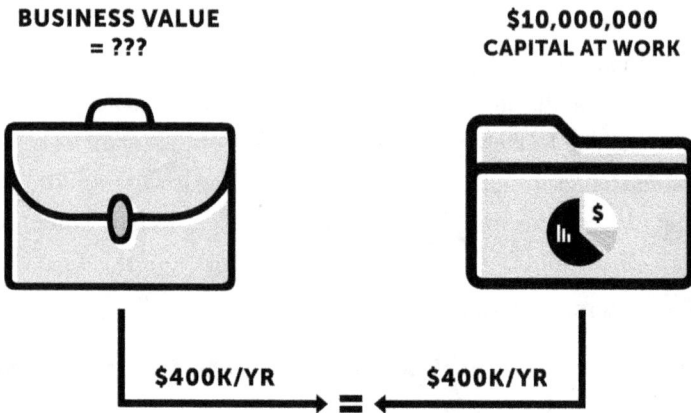

Most business owners (as you likely guessed) are not planning this way.

Why is that? Again, it's because business owners look at their companies as their sole retirement plan. It's their one and only stock. It's their complete 401(k). They work hard for decades, secure in the belief that when it comes time to hang it up and enjoy their golden years, one sale is all it will take to fulfill the needs of their financial future.

For most business owners, however, that's not realistic. In the example we're using, you would need to sell your business for somewhere around $12 million in order for it to fund your entire retirement. That $12 million figure assumes about 20% in taxes, which is quite generous. You would be

---

1   There are all kinds of other details to his theory (e.g., it assumed you invest at least 40% in stocks), but this withdrawal rate will suffice for our example.

extremely lucky to only lose $2 million to taxes on that sale, but it's possible if done correctly. Then, the remaining $10 million would be available to fund the rest of your life's expenditures at a 4% withdrawal rate.

$12 million is a big number, but it looks even bigger when you think about it from the buyer's perspective. You personally make $400,000 per year, so the buyer would have to spend *30 times* your yearly income from the business in order to buy it. The multiple might be a little different depending on how you measure your annual income—by seller's discretionary earnings or by EBITDA (earnings before interest, taxes, depreciation, and amortization)—but the variance doesn't matter enough to change the overarching point: if you are counting on your business sale for retirement, you need a buyer who is willing to wait *decades* before they'll break even.

That doesn't seem very likely, does it? Or asked another way: Would *you* buy another business that would take 10, 20, or 30 years to break even on the deal? Yet, here we are, writing this book because many entrepreneurs walk right into this trap. It's a long walk, too. Year after year, they ignore countless red flags until it's time to retire.

So, how does this happen?

The Stuff Legends Are Made Of

The reason it's easy to ignore those red flags is that everyone thinks their business is going to be the exception, one that gets sold for 30 times earnings or more. Like we said at the beginning of this chapter, we understand that people love, take pride in, and think the world of their companies, and we can completely relate. As entrepreneurs, we should be proud of all we do and the impact we make. The problem is that this pride becomes hubris. Like a slow drip of morphine, this hubris numbs us, year after year—keeping us from thinking accurately and taking action.

Of course, we're also surrounded by legends of entrepreneurs whose hubris was right on the money (literally). Just like we don't see the many, many business owners who fail, we're also seemingly in the midst of an ocean of entrepreneurs who achieved legendary exits.

In fairness, these legends do exist. The companies that make these legends exist, too. They're huge businesses that make strategic acquisitions of other companies, no matter what the financial reports look like. These businesses offer massive multiples—enough to fund 10 retirements—to a handful of lucky business owners. Those fortunate few go on to inspire countless others to not give up on the dream.

The problem is that most of these business owners will not win the entrepreneurial lottery, and a large number neglect proper retirement planning in pursuit of that goal. These entrepreneurs just *know* that one giant, acquisition-hungry company will someday be bidding for their start-up, long before they need to think about retirement.

The truth is that most exits are not nearly as exciting as the ones that make the news. The overwhelming amount of companies are sold for between two and two and a half times the seller's discretionary earnings. At the very high end of what is considered still relatively realistic, owners might sell for up to six times EBITDA. That kind of valuation would still raise eyebrows in most industries, though.

With that in mind, let's revisit our earlier example. You're making $400,000 a year. You need to sell your company for roughly $12 million in order to keep that kind of annual income after retirement. While we know some companies have trouble finding a qualified buyer, we will proceed with the assumption that yours is a ready target for acquisition when you want to sell. If you make

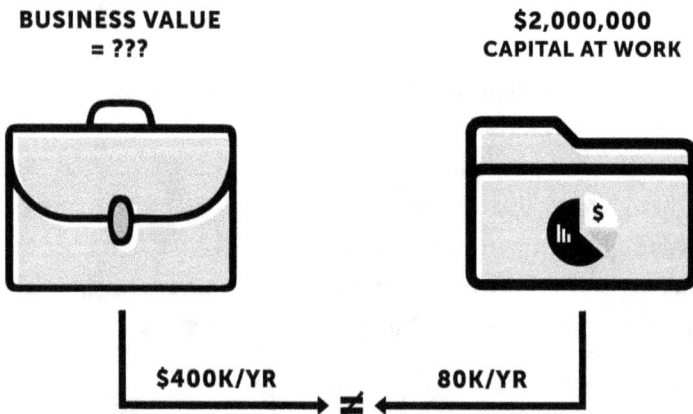

BUSINESS VALUE = ???

$2,000,000 CAPITAL AT WORK

$400K/YR   ≠   80K/YR

$400,000 a year, you are likely going to see a sale price of, at best, about $2.4 million ($400,000 x 6 = $2.4 million). Then there are taxes, but, again, we'll be nice and say the IRS leaves you with $2 million net.

After investing the money from the sale and using the 4% distribution rate we discussed earlier, you will have $80,000 a year for your retirement. That is a giant step down from the $400,000 annual income you enjoyed as a business owner. After selling your company, you'll have to live off one-fifth of what you used to see each year. And remember—that is the *high* end of the multiple most businesses sell for.

What would you do in that situation? Would you decide you'd find a way to make it work on just 20% of what you're accustomed to living on? Would you sit your spouse down to explain this harsh reality? Or would you decide to keep working?

We hear all the time from business owners who are long past the normal age of retirement that they keep working because they absolutely love what they do, and much of the time we believe that truly is the case. However, statistically, we also know that a lot of business owners face the scenario described above, and they choose to keep working because the alternative is unbearable.

It's certainly not an easy decision to make. Most people spend decades planning for their retirement, including those who enjoy their jobs. They look forward to traveling the country—or even the world—spending more time with their grandkids, enjoying their hobbies, and so forth. Then they discover how much they can realistically hope to sell their company for, and—poof—their plans are no longer possible. Gone—just like that—because they failed to look at their business from the buyer's perspective.

The reason many business owners do not sell is that the owners do the math and realize that they can make more money by draining income out of the business for the next several years rather than selling. They'll do this even if it means making other poor decisions like deferring maintenance or capital investment, leaving the company unprepared for the next decade. The owner is just trying to take the most profit possible off the table for a few more years. After that, the hollowed-out business that's left is no longer attractive to a buyer.

Put on Your Buyer's Shoes

Imagine that you're looking at a business that is exactly like yours. The owner might not be quite as good-looking, but everything else is a mirror image of your company. Can you see it?

For this exercise, we are going to stick with the $400,000 salary we've been using, but you can replace that number with how much your company makes you every year.

As the prospective buyer, you've done your due diligence on this mirror company, so you know absolutely everything about it. All the moving parts are laid bare. You have a complete grasp on its payroll. You know the age of its executives. The entire list of important factors is perfectly mapped out inside your mind.

Of course, there are some factors you simply can't know about this business. Those thoughts float into your mind next, as well as the risks involved.

- You may have to work some things out in the business to ensure its continued operation.
- You may have to institute some new training that doesn't currently exist in the company.
- What about the industry? What could happen in the future that would make this a bad investment?
- How do these risks—and others—affect your plans to write a check for this business?

Remember, too, that you're going to do everything possible to press down the value of this company, thus ensuring the lowest possible price for it. After all, you need to recover the costs of buying the company.

With that in mind, how do you feel about buying this business at the high end of the scale? Put another way, how would you feel about paying more than $2 million for your life's work if it was another person's business? It's so important that you make this sobering assessment.

We are not trying to convince you that your company isn't a great place to put your money. We *are* trying to give you the super-realistic perspective on what others would be willing to pay for your company, so you're prepared for the day that it's time to sell.

Prepare for the Probable and You May Still Become a Legend

We hope you see the importance of separating your own financial future from your business's and that you understand the need to accrue wealth over time. We also hope you've been able to take a critical eye to your business and no longer plan to fund your entire retirement with its sale.

At the same time, we didn't intend to dampen your spirits. It's still possible that you become one of those legends other entrepreneurs envy. You may someday get the news that a much larger company is looking to buy yours and is happy to write you a check that's actually heavy from all the ink. But if that's not in the cards, we would much rather you enjoy some extra margin of comfort than suffer the scenario we've seen far too often, wherein business owners never get that legendary buyout amount and end up having to make some excruciating decisions in their old age.

As we discussed earlier in this chapter, it's easy to develop tunnel vision when you're an entrepreneur. Everywhere you look, there seems to be another success story. When you do notice someone fail, it can become all the more reason to believe you're going to become the stuff legends are made of. Your company kept going when others fell and will be the ultimate success. Who wouldn't have those thoughts about something they've dedicated so much of their lives to?

That kind of mindset is probably at least somewhat responsible for entrepreneurs who are able to create successful companies. However, the kind of mindset that leads to a happy, fulfilling life is the one that also knows the prudence of being realistic and planning ahead by creating a stable balance sheet for you and your family.

While this chapter may be sobering, let us be the first to say *congratulations*! You've taken a huge step toward a better financial future. But there are treacherous roads ahead. In the next chapter, we're going to show you common pressures that entrepreneurs experience that lead them away from their business goals.

Chapter 2:
The Siren Song of *More*

Y OU ARE PROBABLY FAMILIAR WITH HOMER'S EPIC POEM THE *ODYS-sey*, even if only from the high school English assignment you didn't read.

The classic tale follows the king of Ithaca, Odysseus, on his 10-year journey home after the Trojan War. (Reflect on that for just a moment . . . the *commute home* gets its own book.) Little did Odysseus and his men realize, as they packed up the spoils of war and boarded their ship, the level of adventure that awaited them on the ride home across the Aegean Sea.

One of the most well-known challenges Odysseus faced was at the hands—or, rather, the voices—of the Sirens. Thanks to the warning of the witch-goddess Circe, Odysseus knew of the Sirens' deadly reputation: These women would sing an enchanting song that no man was able to resist. Unfortunately, that meant many sailors had crashed their ships into the rocks that surrounded these femmes fatales. These men sank beneath the waves, struggling to hear one more note rather than grab another breath.

Nonetheless, Odysseus needed to get home and was already long delayed. (Ten years is a long time to sail all the way around the world, let alone just the Mediterranean.) So, he instructed his men to fill their ears with beeswax so the Sirens' song would have no effect on them. As for Odysseus, he was desperately curious to hear the Sirens' song, so he ordered his men to tie him to the mast of his own ship. As they sailed past the island, the Sirens' song proved as irresistible as legend suggested, and Odysseus struggled furiously to break free. Thankfully his men remained faithful to the plan and bound him tighter, ensuring he couldn't escape to his death.

Are You Sailing Toward the Rocks?

What does the king of Ithaca's terrible travel plans have to do with your finances? Across our careers, we've seen just how easy it is for intelligent people to fall for the personal-finance version of the siren song. One reason is simply that so many other people are right there with them. We make the mistake of looking around, seeing we are surrounded by good company, and relaxing into that feeling of safety. All the while we fail to notice we are sailing closer and closer to the rocks.

For business owners, the siren song is just another version of the one everyone else in society hears—the temptation to always chase more. Our society constantly tells us that what we have is never enough. We cannot be content unless we have more. Yet, of course, once we do have more, the next step is to get even more than that.

So, as business owners, what do most of us do?

- We try to earn more.
- We try to grow our businesses more.
- We try to drive more sales.
- We hire more employees and expand to more locations.
- We try to give our employees more.

Business owners can follow the siren song for decades. The song tells them that, as long as they have their business, they also have a retirement plan. It leads them to believe that when they're finally ready to move on, they'll have the money they need. All they have to do is sell their company.

Of course, you know what happens next: they hit the rocks. They end up no better off than your average executive working for a corporation, even though they ran their own company for decades. The shore is awash with other entrepreneurs who made the same mistake.

Those who heed the call of *more* want to think the Sirens have our best intentions in mind. We tell ourselves that they have lied to everyone else, but we are going to be different. *Our* story will have a happy ending.

It's also easy to forget about all the things that can go wrong over which we have no control. We might be doing everything right, but the unexpected storm could still have the most prudent entrepreneurs needing to sell their company without a solid personal balance sheet to keep them afloat. Lots of these surprise storms are unlikely events, yet unlikely events happen all around us every day. Think of the kinds of unlikely yet possible events that could happen to you and your business. While any one of them is highly unlikely, how likely is it that you make it through the next 20 to 30 years without *at least one* of them impacting your business in some way? You could get sued, even if you did nothing wrong. One of your employees could make a big mistake that hurts your standing with key accounts. Restructuring could change your company's fate. Technological change could erode your competitive advantage. The pendulum of politics may swing in an unfavorable direction for your industry. New regulations or taxes may cripple your growth.

The point is that none of us knows how truly close to the rocks we are. The rocks could seem so far off, and then—*crash!*—one of those unforeseen factors puts your family's security in danger. The more you ignore the call for *more* and focus on your personal financial health, the better off you will be.

The Problem with *More*

Reading the above, you may have thought, "What's wrong with wanting more for my business?" In America, the insatiable drive for more isn't just normal; it's fundamental to success. Indeed, the problem with *more* isn't that it's always a bad goal. It's that, often, it's the only goal. Business owners are lured by this song and have no idea of the peril they are creating for themselves.

Chasing *more* for its own sake isn't a valid indicator of success. We all know of companies that opened a string of new locations right before they went under. We can't tell you how many business owners we've met over the years who have boasted about their growing employee count, how many trucks they'd added to their fleet, or even the new house they'd bought. They had plenty of *more*, and then one day it became too much.

More can also infect our image. Many business owners see the image they give off as a reflection of how successful their companies are. They are not going to walk around wearing numbers for how many employees they have or what their revenue was last year. However, they can drive a nicer car. They can wear an expensive watch. They can take vacations that cost more. On the business side, they begin to obsess over branding, spending far too much because they're afraid the company's image will suffer. Before long, huge amounts of resources are going into decisions that support the company for the company's sake, rather than building the company for the sake of the owner's goals.

When you chase *more* instead of the metrics that really do lead to a better business and a stronger personal balance sheet, the Sirens have you. When you prioritize *more*, it should come as no surprise that it's much easier to spend more in your personal life, too—even when it has nothing to do with your company.

In the last chapter, we talked about the important difference between a business owner and any other type of employee, including executives. Ignoring those differences can be extremely costly.

As an example, an executive at a company may have no problem signing off on $20,000 to send employees to a conference. That covers the airfare, hotel, conference fees, and more. It's not a big deal to the executive because it's not their money. When it's their money—say, for a family vacation—they're a lot slower to pick up the pen and sign a check or start charging things to their credit card.

Business owners sometimes fail to make this distinction. They don't mind spending $20,000 for that conference. However, because they're constantly spending large sums of money like this, their perspective can become distorted. Therefore, they have a much easier time spending $20,000 to make sure their family enjoys a nice vacation together. They might even combine a business trip with a vacation so the business can pay the lion's share. They are already writing these big checks anyway. Plus, all of it's their money, right? This is when *more* can really spiral out of control, and business owners can one day wake up to learn they don't have any *more* to spend.

Revenue vs. Profit

Here's one area where we wouldn't mind seeing a greater number of business owners focusing on *more*. How much money does your business actually make you every year?

We constantly meet with clients who tell us about their revenues. It's $6 million, $8 million, or vaulting to the mid-eight-figure range. Understandably, they're very proud of this number. Revenue is what a lot of business owners hang their hats on more than anything. Then we ask them what they actually take home every year as a business owner. Compared to that $6 to $8 million of revenue, it is not uncommon to hear $250,000 or $300,000.

That's a real problem. What's worse is that if we weren't having these conversations, they'd probably keep chasing *more* without adding anything else to their paychecks. They'd maintain this same massive level of overhead even though their profit is balanced on the knife's edge of those fixed expenses.

Think about the difference between the above example and a business owner with revenues in the $2 million range, but who has an annual income of $700,000. Their company might not sell for as much, but they are able to put a lot more toward their personal balance sheet every single year. Therefore, when it does come time to retire, they don't *need* their company to sell for a massive amount. Meanwhile, the business owner who bragged about much greater revenues (but less in profits) really needs their company to sell at the high end of valuations. Otherwise, they're headed for the rocks.

What would you rather buy? A company that has $20 million of revenue but only nets you $100,000, or one that has just $4 million but gives you $700,000? More revenue won't necessarily mean a higher sales price. Often, businesses that produce the highest incomes also fetch the highest multiples.

Tying Yourself to the Mast

There are a number of ways business owners can take a page out of Odysseus's playbook and prepare themselves for the Sirens. One is to simply surround yourself with reliable people who will hold you accountable. Consider "tying yourself to the mast," thwarting the Sirens before they even get a note out. Set yourself up for success by installing a system that will help you stay on your course when the Sirens' song grows loudest.

There are plenty of ways to tie yourself to the mast, but our favorite has repeatedly proven to be as effective as it is simple—just like rope and a mast. A good friend of the firm, Mike Michalowicz, brought this concept to our attention through his book *Profit First*. Mike is a prolific author on the topic of entrepreneurship and owns a successful consulting company for entrepreneurs. One of the most surprising ways his team helps clients is by encouraging business owners to intentionally create scarcity within their businesses. Specifically, he tells them to extract the money they need personally right away. He warns them not to leave large amounts of cash inside the business's account, because this creates a false sense of abundance. Owners tend to spend more freely when an inflated business account makes them feel secure.

Removing the money immediately does two very important things. The first is obvious. It covers the vital priority of building that personal balance sheet over time. The second is that it keeps the company efficient and scrappy. Pulling out profit first is going to focus the owner's (and their executive team's) minds where they need to be, which is thinking about what kind of life their business is producing for themselves and their families. This kind of thinking leads to the ideal blend of earning potential and freedom.

Remember—financial independence is always built on your personal balance sheet, not on the balance sheet of your business.

Making Yourself Replaceable

If all you do is follow the above instructions to the letter, you'll fare much better than most sailors when they encounter the Sirens.

Of course, in this book we are going to help take your thinking one step further, so you're not set up to achieve just financial independence but *total* independence. Lots of entrepreneurs enjoy healthy cash flow while feeling trapped inside their work schedule. We want you to have the time and locational freedom to really enjoy the fruits of your work!

We are huge fans of Michael Gerber's famous book *The E-Myth Revisited*. If you haven't read it yet, it would be our highly recommended next read, after you finish this book, of course. One of the points Gerber stresses is that you need to be clear about what roles you're performing within your company, because that's the only way you're ever going to be able to hire others to do them.

Figuring out what work you're doing will also help you determine just how much you need to pay yourself and those who take over the roles for you. For example, when you're CEO and owner, you need to think about both of those roles separately and what you need to pay the former to be happy as the latter. You need to say, "As a CEO of my business, I need to make sure that we are producing at least $X amount of cash flow every single year, because that will make me happy as the owner." Now you know the criteria you'll use to measure the next CEO when you replace yourself. This will let you step back from your company—achieving independence—while still maintaining it as a legitimate asset on your personal balance sheet.

Another reason this is so important is that by categorizing those roles—CEO and business owner—you're creating a very helpful form of separation. You operate in both roles, but you're not confusing the two. As a result, you'll find it much easier to resist the siren song that pulls so many business owners away from responsible financial habits and into the shallows of unnecessarily spending money.

"Anybody Can Make a Lot of Money"

We'd like to share another valuable story that was imparted to us by a gentleman whom we first got to know as a client and who then became one of Sound Financial Group's advisors. His name is Jeff Miller, and if you listen to our podcast you can expect to hear even more from him in the future.

Jeff is an exceptionally intelligent guy, as evidenced by the fact that, by his late 40s, he had built up enough assets that work had become optional. When he and his wife, Trisha, came to us, Trisha was still working. She's incredibly intelligent, too, and was on track to become a partner at a globally recognized consulting firm, and was loving every minute of it. Although he never needed to work another day in his life, Jeff shared his wife's drive to be challenged and to find outlets to make an impact in the world. Paul asked him early on, "What if you could do what we do? What if you made this kind of difference working with people, even though you never need to work again?"

"I would love that," he said.

As we continued to work together, one day he shared this story of his grandfather: Decades ago, when Jeff shared news of his latest promotion and salary increase, his grandfather responded, "Don't tell me how much you make, tell me how much you save. Anyone can make a lot of money, not everyone can save it."

Anybody can make a lot of money. Amazing advice and so true.

Unfortunately, most people in our country who discover a way to "make a lot of money" really struggle with saving very much of it. They create a lot of cash flow, but they end up just throwing it back over to someone else's (or some other company's) balance sheet. They spend most of their lives getting swept toward the rocks—all the while looking at their business's balance sheet with satisfaction—until one day it's too late and they sink beneath the waves.

To be clear, we are not suggesting that it's never a good idea to hire more employees, or open a new location, or increase your revenue. Those actions can all be highly beneficial, yet none will lead to a permanent win until you are also regularly contributing to your personal balance sheet. Otherwise, all you're doing is stockpiling value that could get transferred to someone else's balance sheet when you sell your business.

Surround Yourself with Faithful Sailors

If you found this chapter helpful, enlist the help of others. Get a copy to someone you trust and ask them to read it. Maybe it's one of your executives or another employee who has proven to be reliable. Maybe it's your spouse. Share it with anyone you know that will keep you accountable.

Remember, Odysseus—the mighty warrior and king of Ithaca—didn't assume his own self-discipline would be enough. He didn't even think the rope that bound him to the mast would be enough. He got his entire crew together, told them his plan, and made them pledge to do their utmost to ensure he didn't fall for the Sirens' song.

We all need a similar team of faithful confidants around us, because there will be times when the idea of increasing your employee count, buying a new car, or purchasing a vacation home will start singing to you. In the middle of sailing through the crashing waves of life, it can become difficult to see whether those moves are moving you toward your intended goal or toward the rocks.

One of the precautions to take against that kind of risk—which we promise you will encounter at some point—is to have people in your life who will help you. Have an honest conversation where you tell them what your Sirens are and what financial temptations lure you away from the path you know you most desire to follow.

Just as importantly, these trusted individuals can hold you accountable for implementing the systems and structures you need to keep investing in what matters most for your company. Not displays of false abundance, but those investments that will help you grow your business value *and* your personal balance sheet. That's how you'll find true financial independence.

Up to this point, we've spoken in generalities. To best prepare you for the next step in your financial odyssey, we need to dive deeper into the specifics.

In part 2, we'll teach you some of the most effective tactics and strategies that we've learned from advising entrepreneurs like you.

PART 2:
PLAN AHEAD TO ENSURE YOU HAVE ENOUGH

Chapter 3:
Why the Financial Industry Wants You to Retire

"If you first do what seems hard, the rest of your life will be easy."

—Steve D'Annunzio

THE NOTION OF *RETIREMENT* IS NOT THE SAME AROUND THE WORLD, NOR has it been constant in American history. Our culture has come to view retirement as an integral part of life, almost as a biological stage of our lives like puberty or adulthood. However, the concept is newer than you might think.

We only have to go back to the early part of the 1900s to find a different definition for the word *retire*. Back then, we might have *retired* a pair of shoes that had worn out by throwing them away. Or we might have reluctantly *retired* our family's favorite horse when it could no longer perform its duties, which definitely didn't mean sending it to a farm upstate. You can read in books from that era that someone *retired* to the den for the evening. The overarching theme of the word *retirement* was that whatever was being retired was simply of no more use.

Then came Social Security in 1935. This federal government program promised to give Americans some basic support at the end of their lives, so they could afford not to work—at a time when they were probably not able to work that much anyway, thanks to the Great Depression. Benefits started at age 65, at a time when the average life expectancy was only 61 years. Initially you had to outlive the average citizen by four years before you could even start receiving Social Security!

The model worked well, for a while. As the middle class started to grow and companies began rewarding their employees with pensions on top of the Social Security payments from the government, it really did start to feel like a great deal for the average worker. Life expectancy was increasing, and quality of life and overall health were improving as we grew into old age, so a whole generation of workers got behind the idea of "doing their time," knowing they likely had one or more decades to enjoy that guaranteed dual-income stream.

By the 1970s, conditions started to change. Rapidly increasing inflation and steady growth in life expectancy meant Social Security no longer provided enough income to keep people believing "retirement" was possible. It was around that time that we saw financial institutions pick up the retirement flag, and they have been waving it with vigor ever since.

Thus, the 401(k) was born. The promise was simple: invest in these "retirement" accounts every month, and one day you can trade in your button-down for a golf shirt and live the good life. To sweeten the deal, financial institutions offered to help you make sure it turned out perfectly—for a modest set of fees, of course.

Unlike most industries, the financial industry didn't see an unmet need in their market and then seek to create a product to fill it. Instead, they created the products, then set out to create the need.

This is all built around what we call "The Four Rules of Financial Institutions," which is a nearly universal business model for banks and investment firms. They want to:

1. **Get Your Money.** Have you begin depositing money into their products.
2. **Get It Often.** Convince you to deposit more money on a consistent and ongoing basis.

3. **Hold On to It.** Keep the money invested in their products for as long as possible.
4. **Give It Back Slowly.** Release the money back to you as slowly as possible over a long period of time.

It was no accident that the 401(k) became the most prevalent financial product in our country. Most Americans who work for large companies are automatically enrolled in their 401(k) when they are hired, thanks to federal government initiatives to promote such policies. Why? Think about the lobbying we know goes on in Washington every day, particularly by financial institutions. Laws promoting the new 401(k) plans fit the four rules perfectly:

1. Convince the American public that a 401(k) is the first savings tool you should max out.
2. Ensure a contribution is made on every paycheck, plus an employer match.
3. Restrict withdrawals unless the employee leaves the company.
4. The deferred tax nature of the 401(k) means no one is excited to pull large amounts from their 401(k)s and IRAs in any one year, because doing so would rocket them up the tax brackets. Americans have proven so slow to pull money from their 401(k)s and IRAs that the IRS had to institute a rule called "required minimum distributions" (currently at age 72) to ensure we eventually pull money out and pay some taxes on it.

Now let's talk about you: You have spent your career building a company and growing your expertise in a specialized area of knowledge. You are leading teams, creating a powerful identity in the marketplace, and gaining membership in communities where you are highly respected. You have probably been thinking, "Why would I just cut the cord and stop all that while I am still at the top of my game?" That would be a little like teaching your kids to ride their bikes, just so they could check it off the list and never do it again! Maybe you don't want to work quite as many hours, but you don't want to retire in the modern sense of the word. You don't want to stop what you are doing, but you do want to know that you are only doing what you are doing because you love it. You want to be able to stop (or at least pause) doing what you are doing anytime you want and keep living a good life no matter what happens to your business in the future.

If that sounds like you, then instead of pursuing retirement, we encourage you to embrace **Definite Financial Independence (DFI)** as your new target: a state where you no longer rely on your business to support your lifestyle. At that point, you can direct all of your income to assets and live your preferred lifestyle—with or without a steady paycheck.

Wealth Coordination Account

The first step toward DFI is bringing control of your financial activity firmly into your family's hands. The classic move of the sales-driven culture of financial institutions is to find you right at the moment that you discover you have some surplus, and then help you find a place to put that capital. It is a little like the "Leave a Penny/Take a Penny" dish at a convenience store, but their mantra is "Have Some Money? Then Buy Something from Us." We want to help you separate the realization of surplus from the act of buying something, even if that something is a financial product or asset. Creating the habit of setting aside money for the future belongs solely to you (and your spouse), and needs to live as a completely different step from the act of buying a financial product.

You can take back control of your financial future by creating a **Wealth Coordination Account (WCA)**. A WCA is simply a separate checking account at your own bank that you designate for one purpose: to buy assets. Yes, a checking account is a product at a financial institution, but it is imminently liquid. Since you can easily write a check or transfer money electronically when you are ready to deploy your capital, a checking account is still preferable to burying the money in your backyard.

As the diagram below shows, this family makes their WCA the first place they put money each month, the first bill they pay—to themselves— before paying any others. For this family, that means putting 20% of their $400,000 annual income, or $80,000 a year, into their WCA.

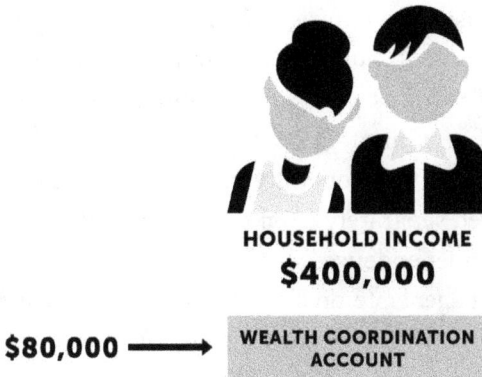

HOUSEHOLD INCOME
$400,000

$80,000 ⟶ WEALTH COORDINATION ACCOUNT

Then, with whatever level of speed works for them, they deploy this money from their WCA into the assets that they choose to buy.

For the sake of this strategy, we define an asset as *anything that can put money in your pocket now, or later, without changing your lifestyle.* That lifestyle distinction is important because money isn't just math. Money is: *math plus human behavior*, and our lifestyle is the most powerfully ingrained part of our behavior. The assets you choose to invest in might be rental real estate, a commercial building, certain kinds of

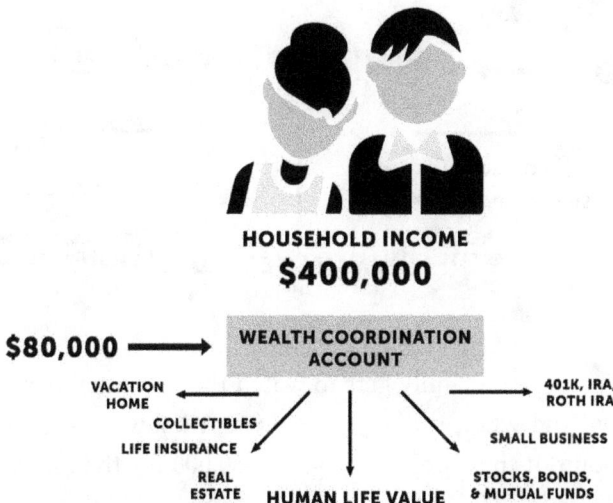

HOUSEHOLD INCOME
$400,000

$80,000 ⟶ WEALTH COORDINATION ACCOUNT

VACATION HOME
COLLECTIBLES
LIFE INSURANCE
REAL ESTATE
HUMAN LIFE VALUE
401K, IRA, ROTH IRA
SMALL BUSINESS
STOCKS, BONDS, & MUTUAL FUNDS

life insurance, other business ventures, or the classic stocks/bonds/mutual funds. One item you will notice is not on this list is your primary residence, otherwise known as your home. Your home is so tied into the lifestyle choices of a family that it doesn't get to operate as a cold hard asset. Yes, your home will hopefully grow as an item of value, but it needs to be considered separately from the strategy of building assets for Definite Financial Independence.

Whenever your assets generate dividends or passive income, or are liquidated for gain, deposit that cash back into your WCA until you create a strategy for its next deployment, so each dollar that goes into the WCA is really planted like a seed that gets to experience compound growth over time.

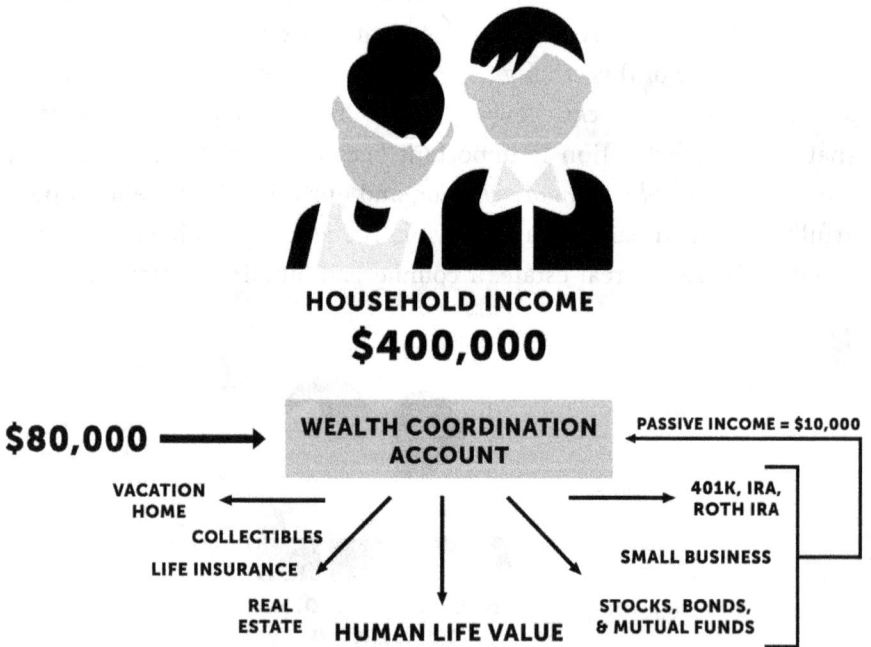

HOUSEHOLD INCOME
$400,000

$80,000 ⟶   **WEALTH COORDINATION ACCOUNT**   ⟵ PASSIVE INCOME = $10,000

VACATION HOME ⟵   401K, IRA, ROTH IRA ⟶

COLLECTIBLES

LIFE INSURANCE

SMALL BUSINESS

REAL ESTATE   **HUMAN LIFE VALUE**   STOCKS, BONDS, & MUTUAL FUNDS

As time passes, the family gets to watch that potential passive income stream grow, and when it reaches $320,000, they will have hit a special inflection point. If they are setting aside $80,000 for the future each year,

$320,000 represents everything they were living off of for their lifestyle—taxes, mortgage, vacations, eating out, and more. When their WCA shows them the capacity to fund that level of income from their assets, they have officially reached Definite Financial Independence.

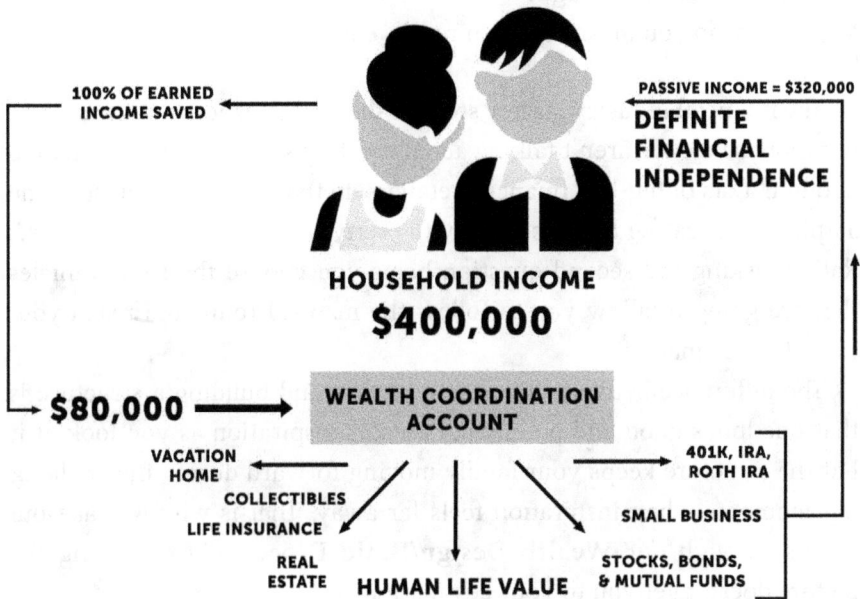

At this point, they could make the choice to stop working and live off their assets. They could also choose to do exactly the kind of work that is most exciting and fulfilling to them, depositing 100% of whatever income they might make into their WCA, while supporting their lifestyle from their assets. No matter what they choose, they have achieved a work-optional lifestyle, with the freedom to decline to do all the things they never enjoyed doing but had to. The only difference is that they are now living off of their passive income and buying all of their new assets (or creating additional surplus) with their earned income.

Sufficiency, Surplus, and Superfluence

Now that we have the Wealth Coordination Account as a system to help you map out your progress, we can start to look at where you might want to go. To figure that out, we have two very important questions for you to consider:

1. How much is enough?
2. How do you make sure you reach "enough"?

The financial industry largely stops at the first question, but the second question is key. We aren't talking about creating some sort of road map to "enough." Lots of big-box financial retailers do that. (Haven't you seen the 50-plus-page leather binders filled with pretty colored graphs and charts?) Rather, asking the second question helps you choose the right vehicles that are going to allow you to follow the mapped route and reach your intended destination.

The difference between drawing a picture and building a structure is that one looks good and potentially creates inspiration as you look at it, but the structure keeps your family moving forward during the challenging moments when inspiration feels far away. That is why we take our clients through our **Wealth Design/Build Process**—just drawing the picture doesn't get you to your destination.

While most people do ask the first question, they often don't know how to accurately determine how much will be enough for a lifestyle that will bring them happiness. Therefore, they simply chase a cookie-cutter number they receive from financial advisors or one of countless online calculators that end up doing more harm than good. This number is generally so high that people begin to panic. They realize they'll never be able to hit this amount—and, therefore, are doomed to a miserable life—so they start taking risks.

In the 1990s, a lot of people in this position bought up tech stocks as the advent of the internet seemed to promise that a good idea and a URL were all you needed for unlimited growth. In the early 2000s, it was real estate that promised lifelong rewards for those who went all in. In both cases, this reckless get-rich-quick strategy only made the problem worse.

Both real estate and stocks can be useful tools for securing our wealth over the long term. The problem comes when you adopt a fear-based approach, swinging for that big magic number. Ironically, it's the very way this magic number was pursued that ensured it would not be reached.

In the remainder of this chapter, we are going to introduce you to a much better way of determining your magic number, first by helping you see that it isn't *one* magic number, but two or three. Once you understand this concept, you'll know what will be *sufficient* for you, what it will take to enjoy a lifestyle of *surplus*, and where to aim if you are actually after *superfluence*. No panic, anxiety, or feelings of doom required.

1. Sufficiency: What Is a Good Life for You?

Sufficiency refers to having slightly more than the amount you need to enjoy a good life. This is likely an amount that the majority of you have already surpassed. Sufficiency is not a life of luxury, but a life that is "good enough" and distances you from any unacceptable compromises. The key questions for you might be:

- What size home is sufficient for your family?
- What kind of neighborhood would be sufficiently safe?
- What is a sufficient school system?
- What kinds of vacations are sufficient?

The answers to these questions should not reflect your ideal situation. Your dream home is most likely much bigger than one that is *sufficient*. At the same time, we're not suggesting you aim at the bare minimum of "just surviving," either. Your family could survive in a home that is much smaller than the one you consider sufficient.

Another way to think about sufficiency is that it's having $1 more than you need before you'd have to consider making some otherwise unthinkable compromises. In other words, sufficiency is a life with some compromises, but without any compromises you are unwilling to make.

As you can imagine, this amount differs greatly for everyone, which is why those cookie-cutter financial product solutions fail. Someone who's been making $10 million a year for 20 years probably has a very different definition of "unacceptable compromises" compared to someone who's been making $100,000 for the past couple of years. This is why we emphasize over and over to clients how important it is that they complete a personal inventory to find out what these numbers are for their family.

If you are reading this book, then you are likely already living a lifestyle that meets or exceeds your sufficiency. When you look around, you like the home you own, the neighborhood you live in, and the car you drive. Your business currently creates enough cash flow to give you a good life. You may not have reached the apex of your earnings potential, but you are content.

Many people have the wrong idea about being content. They worry that being content means losing their ambition. They even avoid the feeling of contentment altogether—for fear that appreciating their mid-level sedan will mean never owning a high-end luxury import. If this sounds familiar, don't worry, that is only because it is a very common default mindset in our culture.

In 1971, Brickman and Campbell introduced the world to the "hedonic treadmill" in their famous essay, "Hedonic Relativism and Planning the Good Society." This treadmill refers to the human tendency to quickly adapt to new improvements in our lives and then settle back down to our normal level of happiness. To get that former rush, we have to constantly find new improvements, often by purchasing them. But the new level of happiness never lasts. Like a treadmill, we can find we are working harder and harder just to stay in one place.

The gigantic and prolific marketing and social media machines (which more and more seem like one and the same) know all about the hedonic treadmill. Cultivating contentment takes a lot of work, more so because we receive very little help from outside sources. After all, who do you think Madison Avenue prefers to sell to—those who are content or those who constantly need *more*?

If you're reading this, chances are it's because, at some point, you decided the job you had, or the industry you were in, or the money you made—or some combination of all three—wasn't good enough. That's why you set out to start your own company. Whatever motivated you, continue to use that drive. Be ambitious and look for new opportunities, but don't let that keep you from cultivating contentment. Don't let ambition keep you from understanding where your threshold for "good enough" is, or you may actually find yourself falling far below it. (If you would like a great book that delves into this topic even further, one we recommend is *Satisfied* by Jeff Manion.)

Another peril of the hedonic treadmill is the constant pursuit of goals that don't lead to a life of satisfaction. Sufficiency is not burying your ambitions; it simply means securing your ambitions in order, and with greater permanence. Earlier in life, you might have had an ambition to let your family go to the grocery store and not have to do any mental math before rolling the cart to the checkout line. The potential embarrassment of needing to put an item back became unacceptable to you, so you eliminated that compromise. It has probably been a long time since you didn't have enough money to walk out with all of your groceries, and the longer it has been, the more painful it would be to go back.

We want you to have strong ambitions and a big vision for the future—we want that for ourselves, too—and we have discovered there is an order of operations at work! We start with sufficiency first so that we can earn the right to take risks, knowing our core needs will be cared for. To achieve that we have to define and secure this number before moving on to the next two levels.

Almost everyone skips this step, but please don't move on to the next section until you understand what that sufficiency number is for you and why it's so important . Before you read the next section, please sit down with your spouse (if you have one) and define the sufficiency income for your family. Include plenty of details, too. For example, maybe sufficiency would mean a smaller home and downsizing to just one vehicle. That doesn't mean we want you to actually make those changes. We just want you to discover the comfort and security that comes from finding out what that sufficiency level would look like for your family.

As a cautionary tale, consider the following story of a man who took sufficiency for granted:

Before the tech bubble reached its apex in March 2000, this man (who shall remain anonymous) won the lottery in the form of an amazingly lucrative tech company exit and built himself to billionaire status through investment in real estate. When the Great Recession hit, his net worth went from just north of $1 billion down to zero in a matter of months.

How do we know this story? The former billionaire interviewed with one of our friends for a sales job. Imagine that: going from having more than a billion dollars to updating your resume in just a few months.

To his credit, the man was very open about his past and the mistakes he made that led him to the interview. At one point, our friend asked him, "Before this all happened, when you were still a billionaire, how hard would it have been for you to have taken a small percentage of your net worth—say, 5%, $50 million—and just set it aside in something extremely low risk?"

"Not hard at all," the man replied. "I probably wouldn't have even noticed the difference."

Our friend then asked, somewhat carefully, "What would that $50 million mean to you now?"

In a quiet pause in the conversation, the man's eyes filled with tears, and he responded, "It would be everything to me now."

We never want you to star in that kind of story. We never want you to become a cautionary tale. So please be sure to define sufficiency for your family right here and now, before it's too late.

2. Surplus: What Does Your Future Look Like?

The easiest way to define surplus is a good life with some luxuries and things that are nice to have. This is what most people are aiming for. It's the magic number they get from a cookie-cutter financial advisor or dubious online resource.

As we covered earlier, aiming for this number without establishing sufficiency first is a fool's errand. Those that do reach it often end up in a similar situation as the billionaire we just told you about. They never discovered what sufficiency meant to them, so they never actually created and protected that baseline.

Unfortunately, this means that when they fall, they have nothing to catch them. There's no safety net. There's no "good enough" mercifully waiting for them, and they may even end up buried by debts they can't manage. Having surplus is a fantastic place to be, and it's a dangerous goal to aim for without achieving sufficiency first.

Many of you reading have probably already achieved some degree of surplus, in terms of your annual cash flow from your business. However, most of you probably aren't in a place where you could maintain a surplus lifestyle if your business went away. Do you remember all those risk factors we covered in the last section? If one of those were to unexpectedly compromise your business, would you still be able to live a lifestyle of surplus? If not, you can simply go back and plan for sufficiency. It's not too late.

If you are ready for surplus, here's what we'd suggest. When clients first come to our firm for help, most of them have already experienced some amount of going through ups and downs with their finances.

PATH OF CURRENT STRATEGY

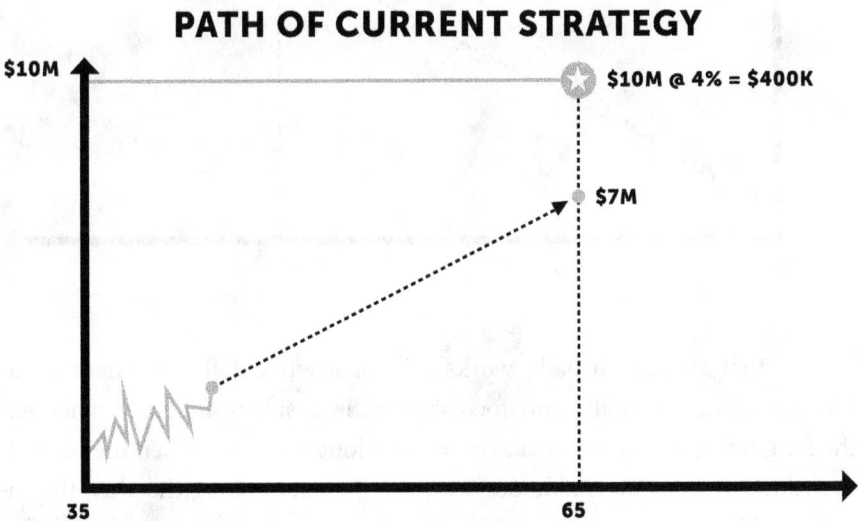

$10M

$10M @ 4% = $400K

$7M

35   65

The following example demonstrates how merely achieving a life of sufficiency is jeopardized when we don't follow the order of operations.

For our example, let's assume a couple has a goal of retiring with $400,000 of annual income. Remember the 4% rule we covered in chapter 1? At a 4% distribution rate, they'll need $10 million in assets in order to accomplish this goal. Of course, when they start building projections based on where they currently are with their financial planning (again, before they meet us), they might realize that their investments are only on track to reach $7 million. This is when they decide it's worth taking more risks. It's the only way they can see themselves hitting that $10 million they must have for the future they want.

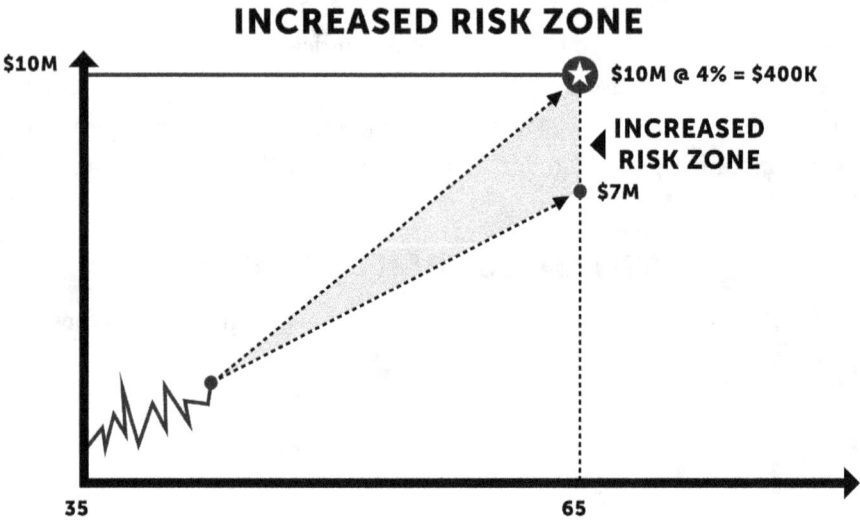

INCREASED RISK ZONE

And that strategy usually works . . . for a while. Often in these situations, investors are really only focusing on the upside result they want over the long term, not the downside potential along the way. When the market cycles through an inevitable downward adjustment along the way, the investor realizes after the fact that their new, riskier portfolio is too much for them to handle. Once again, they react by altering their investment strategy dramatically. Now, instead of taking on more risk, they're buckling down and going into protection mode. They just want to conserve what they have left before any more mistakes hurt their savings further.

PATH OF CURRENT STRATEGY

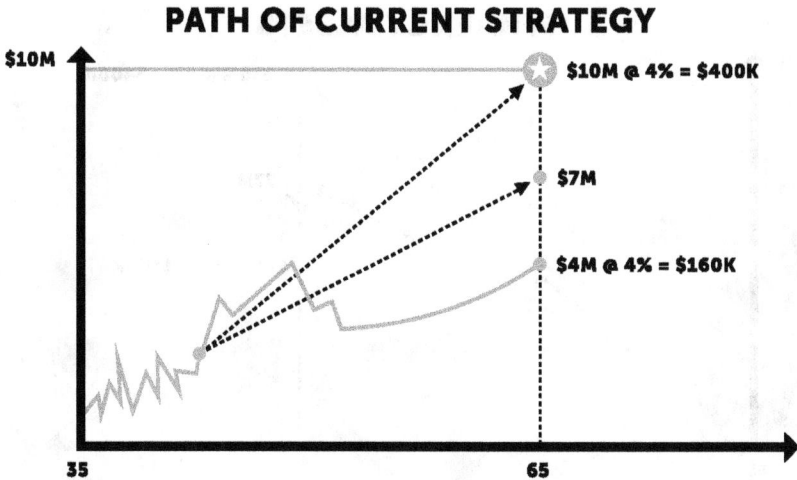

$10M

$10M @ 4% = $400K

$7M

$4M @ 4% = $160K

35

65

As a result, they fall from $10 million all the way down to $4 million. Of course, $4 million is still a lot of money. However, it's not the amount the client wanted. It's not the total they needed to enjoy their desired type of life after retirement.

With $4 million in assets, they'll only see $160,000 a year in income. That's not even half of the $400,000 they need to live a life of surplus, and definitely less than their sufficiency number. Put yourself in this person's shoes: Imagine what that would feel like to approach retirement knowing you need to go through the plans you and your spouse had made—for 20, 30, maybe even close to 40 years—and now need to start deciding which unwanted compromises you have to accept, which parts of your dream to give up.

The real problem is that this person never distinguished their sufficiency in the beginning. Now they are dealing with a significant amount of unwanted compromise . . . for the rest of their life.

That can be a tough mental exercise to go through, but it's definitely a lot better than the alternative—actually experiencing the reality of it. Our friend and business coach Steve D'Annunzio calls this the *Hard-Easy*: If you first do what seems easy, the rest of your life will be hard. If you first do what seems hard, the rest of your life will be easy.

SUFFICIENCY ASSETS

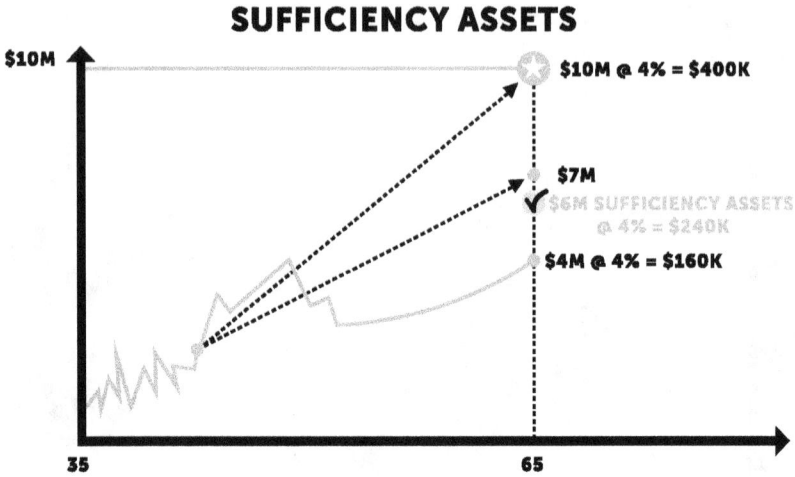

$10M @ 4% = $400K

$7M

$6M SUFFICIENCY ASSETS @ 4% = $240K

$4M @ 4% = $160K

$10M

35   65

To ensure that you never need to experience unwanted compromise in your lifestyle, pursue surplus with an awareness of your sufficiency. By first determining your sufficiency, you have the luxury of making some very different decisions about retirement.

When clients begin working with us, we start by helping them determine what sufficiency means for them. For the couple in our example, sufficiency can be secured living on $240,000 a year. At our 4% distribution rate, that requires $6 million of assets accumulated on their personal balance sheet.

Is it the same life they would live on $400,000? No, they enjoy as much luxury, and some compromises will be made. But that $240,000 is sufficient to keep them from having to make any compromises they would deem unacceptable.

With their sufficiency secured, they can go out and make surplus investments, those investments that have more volatility . . . and more upside. But these riskier strategies are only funded with assets above and beyond the assets needed to reliably produce sufficiency income. Those riskier investments now have a greater likelihood of success, too: when you have your sufficiency secured, you are likely to make better decisions during both good times and challenging times, because you have the con-

COURSE OF CLARITY™

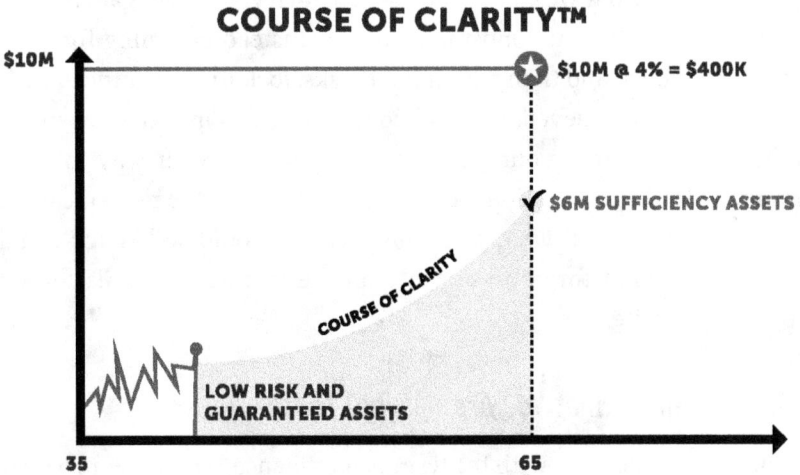

$10M

⭐ $10M @ 4% = $400K

✔ $6M SUFFICIENCY ASSETS

COURSE OF CLARITY

LOW RISK AND
GUARANTEED ASSETS

35   65

fidence, the security, and the certainty that you will not have to make
unacceptable compromises now or in the future.

COURSE OF CLARITY™

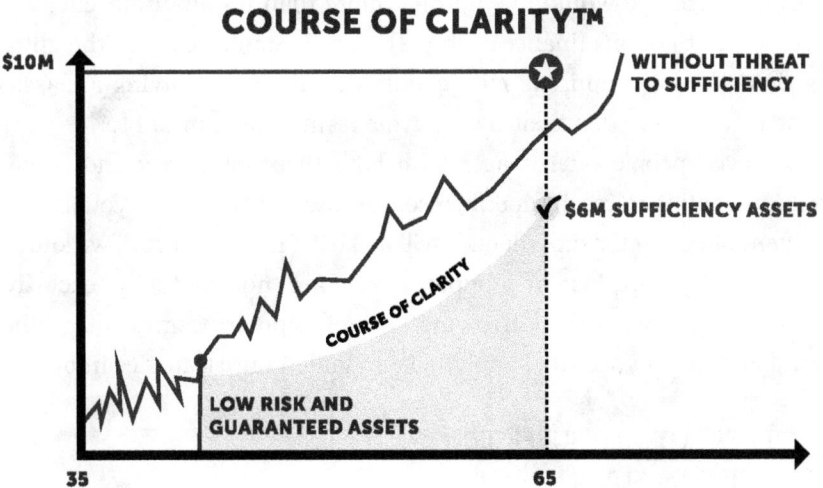

$10M

⭐ WITHOUT THREAT
TO SUFFICIENCY

✔ $6M SUFFICIENCY ASSETS

COURSE OF CLARITY

LOW RISK AND
GUARANTEED ASSETS

35   65

By creating what we call a **Course of Clarity**, you will gain a massive advantage over the route most people take. Instead of aiming for surplus first, falling short, and then taking huge risks, lock in your sufficiency first. With sufficiency achieved, you and your spouse can introduce as much or as little volatility into your strategy as you like on your way to surplus. Just like with the last section, before you move on to the next, please take some time to map out what a surplus lifestyle would be like for you and your family. Don't forget to dig into all the important details for every aspect of your life.

3. Superfluence: What You Are (Maybe) Shooting For

You may not be familiar with the term "superfluence," but if you're like most entrepreneurs we've met, you're very familiar with the goal it defines.

Superfluence is what we refer to as "100-foot-yacht money." It's the level of wealth people reach after a legendary exit—the kind that makes the news. It's what happens when your executive assistant tells you a "Mr. Bezos" would like to sit down with you ASAP and will be bringing his checkbook.

At our firm, we would like nothing more than for all of our clients to become what famous finance author Thomas J. Stanley called, "the glittering rich." We have no issue with clients who dream of buying a massive yacht someday or even their own private island they can sail to.

However, people often wager with both their sufficiency and surplus while attempting to reach superfluence. Because, we hate to tell you this, not everyone shooting for superfluence will make it. (You're shocked, we know.)

Sufficiency, surplus, and superfluence are not mutually exclusive, though, despite what the harrowing tales of popular business magazines would like to tell you. You simply have to build your strategies in order:

- PROTECT your SUFFICIENCY
- BUILD for SURPLUS
- SHOOT for SUPERFLUENCE
- AND NEVER COMPROMISE SUFFICIENCY

Still, plenty of our clients have no interest in reaching the level of superfluence. These business owners—and there are a number of them—have no intention of joining "the glittering rich." Rather, they master the art of contentment, achieve sufficiency, and enjoy a surplus lifestyle.

Superfluence may not be for you, and that's perfectly fine. As we mentioned in the section "Securing Sufficiency and Protecting Your Future," the key is setting your goals consciously. Many people chase 100-foot-yacht money unconsciously, because they've never sat down and thought about what they want their life to look like and what really matters to them. They just assume that would be fantastic, so they work themselves past the point of surplus, eventually take their new boat out on the water, and think, "Is this what I worked so hard for?"

As before, we encourage you to take some time to think about what you want and discuss the topic with your family. Maybe you do have some really lofty, own-your-own-island type goals. If you do, get specific about them. Map out the details and make sure your spouse (if you have one) is on board.

Know What You Want

When you establish contentment, when you really know where that is, you become almost completely immune to the kind of advertising that attempts to make you spend money on things you don't want. Going forward, you'll be able to make financial decisions based on the goals that you've consciously decided on. Instead of what some advertising agency decided you need.

Before you jump into the next chapter, please take some action to help this book be more than just an entertaining read. Make an investment in a better future for you and your family by simply defining what sufficiency, surplus, and superfluence look like for *you*. Once you've done that, we can begin taking some more concrete steps toward that ultimate goal: a successful balance sheet for you, not just your business.

(You can find the worksheet we built to help you look at your sufficiency, surplus, and superfluence by going to *www.YBYWbook.com*.)

Chapter 4:
Why You Have to Build Your Own Balance Sheet

NTREPRENEURS SHARE A FEW KEY CHARACTERISTICS. CAROLINE Adams Miller says in her book *Getting Grit: The Evidence-Based Approach to Cultivating Passion, Perseverance, and Purpose* (Sounds True, 2017) that entrepreneurs have to possess a vision for the future and a high level of tenacious ambition to sustain the level of grit required to launch their business and grow it successfully.

Because they have created something wonderful, often out of nothing, most entrepreneurs possess a strong sense of pride toward their companies, and that pride is well deserved! Entrepreneurs are a very small group who create massive positive change in their communities, countries, and even across the entire globe.

In all of our years working with entrepreneurs, we see most fail to apply their incredible business skills to their own finances and their own personal balance sheet. Instead of using that same ambition, vision, and work ethic to *also* build a personal balance sheet that's as strong as their business's balance sheet, entrepreneurs tend to maintain a singular focus on the business long after that focus ceases to serve their goals. This chapter is about directing your formidable talents toward your own health and happiness.

What Everyone Knows that Most Business Owners Do Not

Imagine your friend works as an executive for a giant technology company. They love it there and all signs are pointing in the right direction for the company itself. It may never make the news for a legendary buyout, but it's certainly going to be a success.

One day they reveal to you that their entire investment portfolio is invested in only one stock, in only one company, which happens to be the same company that pays their salary. They have millions of dollars in this company's stock. When you politely press on the issue, they don't understand your concern. Haven't you heard how well it's doing? Isn't it completely obvious? This company is taking off—has taken off—and it's only going to keep climbing. They tell you they have no plans to change their investment strategy. From now until retirement, they'll continue to buy stock in the company. Then, when it's time to retire, they'll sell and enjoy the good life.

The above scenario may seem too absurd to even consider. No matter how much income they make, or how successful the company is that they work for, everyone from their summer intern to the CEO of their company would be able to tell them this is a terrible investment strategy, and they are putting their entire future at risk. Who would place their whole financial future in the hands of just one stock, especially in the company they also work for? They are literally banking all of their income *and* their assets on a single bet.

We have seen this happen time and again, and if you know enough corporate executives, you also likely know someone who is or has been in this position. They are all highly intelligent, accomplished professionals, yet they pursue a personal financial strategy that no professional advisor or business book would support.

Paradoxically, it's often the smartest and most successful business owners who fall into this trap. The less successful owners usually have a much easier time finding other places to put their money. As much as they love their business, they know when a boat has holes in it. Therefore, they start looking for other places to put their money. To a successful business owner, investing in anything *but* the business can seem almost akin to cowardice. You've worked hard on building a successful business. You plan to continue building a company that accomplishes more and more every year. If you have complete confidence in your business's future, why would you invest your money anywhere else? Isn't that a sign of doubt?

We brought up one reason back in chapter 2: we can't predict everything. Remember Blockbuster? They are certainly easy to shake our collective heads at now, as a cautionary tale of not keeping up with the times, but can't you remember (not all that long ago) when it was hard to find a person who *didn't* have a Blockbuster card?

Confidence in our businesses and our own abilities is important; blind confidence can lead to poor decision-making. Spreading your investment portfolio beyond your company is not admitting any shred of doubt in yourself or in your business; it is taking a stand that one bad choice by an employee, new regulations, or innovative technology *will not* destroy your balance sheet.

Put another way, building your own balance sheet is not a lack of confidence in your company, it is simply acting in a way that is in alignment with what we call **the two fundamental financial mechanics of an entrepreneur's life**:

1. You will never have financial independence on the business balance sheet; independence only ever occurs on your personal balance sheet.
2. One day, by design or by default . . . you will not own the business you own today.

Accepting the truth of these two statements is not a surrender. If we accept that your company is not likely to sell for enough to net the level of assets required to supply your income for a lifetime (remember the business would need to sell for 25 times EBITDA, and you wouldn't buy it for that much yourself, if the tables were turned), you must *already* have other money on your balance sheet to move into financial independence after selling your business.

The tech executive friend of yours in the scenario above is actually in a superior position than business owners who have nothing on their personal balance sheet. That friend can at least divest themselves of their single-stock position over time. They don't need to sell every share at one price, hoping it's the best they'll ever see. They can slowly divest themselves and move the money into better investments. They can also liquidate in a very short period of time if necessary. As a business owner, this kind of flexibility does not exist.

Everyone Thinks They're the Exception

Have you ever heard of *illusory superiority*?

In chapter 1, we discussed why entrepreneurs are exceptional. We are a unique breed. We don't have a "boss." Every day we work to create a vision of the future and bring it closer to reality. Our businesses have survived difficulties that would cause other people to walk away, and this is just another day. Yet, for some reason, our own personal balance sheet and financial management practices are far below average, and we can't see it. Why?

Illusory superiority is a psychological term that describes how the vast majority of people think they are better than others in most areas of life. For example, in a classic study carried out by K. Patricia Cross in 1977, 94% of college professors reported that they believed their IQ was above average compared to their peers.

Professors aren't the only ones, either. Study after study has shown that almost any time people are asked where they rank relative to others, the vast majority of us will choose "above average." When you combine this natural inclination with the pride we business owners feel for our companies, it's only natural that we'd become the equivalent of single-stock investors.

Illusory superiority is hard for us to identify in the present, and even harder to recognize into the future. In general we don't have enough facts (in other words, crystal balls) to know what our businesses (or the buyers' market) will look like 10 years in the future, but we have confidence, so we assume a very high multiple.

What we do know from chapter 1 is that you are unlikely to sell your business for an amount that will provide the income to support everything you need for the rest of your life. We must fight our own illusory superiority if we are to build productive personal balance sheets that will secure our financial futures.

The Personal Balance Sheet You Need to Retire

Several times, we've referenced the 4% distribution rate that many financial advisors recommend. It's considered the rule of thumb for retirement planning for most people. We use it because it's a good general guideline and makes concepts easy to explain. However, we would never recommend that you apply the 4% rule or any other "rule of thumb" to your specific retirement planning without diving deep into your specific situation and unique goals.

One of the most common pieces of advice we hear from financial advisors and the media is that you need 70% of your pre-retirement income to live on after you quit working. Maybe you have heard something similar over the years, but have you ever examined that advice?

Currently, when do you typically spend more money: during the week while you are working, or on the weekend? Do you usually spend more money when you are at home, or when you are on vacation? When you retire, every day will be like a weekend, and you will probably have the opportunity to take a lot more vacations, too!

You can probably think of more reasons for spending the same amount, if not more money, after you leave your business, but here's a big one: Consider all the personal spending you have been able to run through the business that the IRS will no longer allow you to deduct. How much would just that single change on your tax return increase your out-of-pocket personal lifestyle cost?

Financial advisors too often assume we will spend significantly less when we retire than we do now. Despite a permanent-weekend lifestyle, they keep coming back to that 70% range of what we are currently making. Also, as you've probably noticed, one of the recurring themes in this book is that you, as a business owner, are not remotely the same as an employee—even a high-paid executive.

The kind of advice you hear from most financial advisors—or on the other end of a Google search—is directed at 99% of the population. As entrepreneurs, all of us are part of the 1% who must think differently or risk putting off retirement indefinitely. Therefore, while we may reference some conventional rules from time to time in this book, do not assume these to be accurate for your situation. Rather we invite you to use them as a way to explore the principles they reveal.

Designing Your Business to Achieve Definite Financial Independence

As we explained earlier in the book, the final stage of business planning is what we call the "design stage," and it involves converting wealth from your business balance sheet to your personal balance sheet. While your business is still a very important investment—probably the one that will give you the highest return—*your business can only be that highest return-ing investment if it is not your only investment.* In order to identify what other investments and assets you need to add to your personal balance sheet, we must first identify your **Enterprise Capital Gap**.

Your Enterprise Capital Gap is the difference between the amount of money you can sell your business for and the total amount of assets you need to live the lifestyle you want during retirement. In the example we've been using, the Enterprise Capital Gap is:

- $10 million (the amount you need for $400,000 a year at the 4% distribution rate)—$2 million after tax (the amount you can sell your business for at $400,000 x 6, a high but achievable multiple) = an Enterprise Capital Gap of $8 million. If you already have $3 million of capital at work on your balance sheet, you have a $5 million gap between you and Definite Financial Independence (DFI).

To close this $5 million gap, you need to set aside a portion of your income every year on a consistent, ongoing basis—just like non-business owners do with their 401(k)s and other retirement accounts.

The money you set aside is used to purchase *assets*. However, the term "asset" is often too loosely defined. We define an asset as *anything that puts*

ENTERPRISE CAPITAL GAP WORKSHEET

SOUND Financial Group

Often owners have imagined what their business would sell for, and that it would "be enough". Sometimes it is. Most of the time it is not, but we don't realize it, because the people who didn't sell their businesses successfully are not hanging out in the communities you spend time in as a successful business owner. The calculations below are not meant to impugn or diminish the value of your business, rather to help you think accurately about how much your personal balance sheet must grow to bring you to DFI.

Remember: You will never build financial independence on your Business Balance Sheet. Your financial independence will always come from the strength of your personal balance sheet.

	EXAMPLE	NOTES	YOUR BUSINESS
Last Year Total Revenue	$4,000,000	Top line gross revenue	
Last Year Owner Income (For smaller businesses, use Seller's Discretionary Earnings or EBITDA)	$400,000	Current Business Cash Flow you take into your household, not counting re-investment in the business	
Owner Profit Margin	10%	Remember: Most buyers are buying your business for an income stream.	
Conservative Profit Multiple For Valuation in a sale	6	Depending on the Industry and other factors, typical sales price valuations are in a range of 2.5X-6X SDE or EBITDA	
Sale Price	$2,400,000	We are ignoring taxes for the moment. Rest assured all numbers below likley get smaller after tax	
Estimated Tax to be Paid	$400,000	Estimated Tax on Sale of Business	
Net Cash Proceeds on Sale	$2,000,000	Net Cash Proceeds on Sale	
Annual Income Draw from Assets in Retirement	4%	"The 4% Rule" comes from a study done by Trinity University in Texas, and has become the industry conversation starter around taking income from our assets in retirement	
Annual Retirement Income from Business Sale	$80,000	Annual Retirement Income from Business Sale	
ENTERPRISE CAPITAL GAP	$8,000,000	The additional assets needed to create the same amount of owner income post-sale	
Amount of assets required to generate income equal to the business		Take the amount of current income you are earning in salary and K-1 from your business and divide by 4% (.04)	
Current Capital At Work	$3,000,000	Current Capital At Work -- IRA, 401(k), Investment Accounts, DO NOT include Primary Residence	
DFI Gap	$5,000,000	Subtract the Your current Capital at Work from Amount of Asset required	

If you think it would be valuable to get help in building your Personal Balance Sheet, reach out to us and we would be happy to schedule a Philosophy Conversation with you.

money in your pocket now or has the ability to do so in the future, without changing your lifestyle.

This strategy—plus the $2.4 million exit—will give you sufficient funds for the golden years you've always dreamed of enjoying.

(You can request an editable Excel and PDF copy of our Enterprise Capital Gap worksheet at *YBYWBook.com*.)

Let's take this a step further and assume your business makes you $600,000 a year. At a 4% distribution rate, you'll need $15 million to replace that $600,000. To have $15 million after taxes, you'll need a buyer willing to pay about 32 times annual earnings. We know that is not likely to happen.

Remember, just keep asking yourself: Would *you* absorb a competitor through acquisition if you had to pay the seller 32 times their owner profit for the privilege? Probably not. At $600,000 in annual income, a more realistic price for your business is probably $3 million. After taxes, you'll be at around $2.4 million. That's a lot of money, but it's also $12.6 million short of where you wanted to be for retirement. At a 4% distribution rate, $2.4 million will only give you $96,000 a year. Even if you go with the rule of thumb we mentioned above—70% of pre-retirement income—you're still more than $300,000 short per year.

When we are onstage at business conferences, right at this point we see a crowd of faces turn ashen. There is a sea of business owners who never considered this, and now they're starting to worry. They realize they have not been focusing on the one thing responsible for their financial independence: their personal balance sheet.

Your business is just one investment of many that you need to build your personal balance sheet. Therefore, your balance sheet must be built in coordination with your company's value. This means you need to understand what that value is and not allow your pride in your company—albeit understandable—decide for you.

This is where we get some great advice from Paul's father, Lee Adams. When trading baseball cards as a child, Paul would diligently look up every value in the *Beckett Monthly* and state proudly what his most valuable card was worth. Lee would always reply, "That card is only worth that much after someone has paid you for it." Truer words have rarely been spoken.

Remember, it's not how much you want to sell it for that matters. It's how much someone will buy it for that will determine its actual worth.

Knowing that, how do we transfer wealth from our business balance sheet to our personal balance sheet? One of the most important things we can do comes from our colleague Alan Chaffee of Turning Point Consulting in Seattle. Alan insists that we should not own or run a business if it's not producing a profit enough to also build up your personal balance sheet. Put in another way, you don't want a high-paying job if it means incurring capital and personal balance sheet risk.

As a business owner, your company should provide you with a significant amount of reward for taking that kind of risk. How do you do this? It's actually quite simple, in theory. As an owner, you give yourself a paycheck for your work as an employee. Then, the next check you write to yourself should be the amount of the profit you are entitled to as the business owner.

Let's say your goal is 20% profitability. That is what you take right off the table and out of your business's balance sheet. Do not leave that money inside the business! This is extremely important: the business checking account might seem like a great place to keep your excess cash, but we guarantee that hoarding cash there will not produce the best outcomes for your business *or* your personal balance sheet.

Aside from the benefit of ensuring that money is regularly going where it ultimately needs to grow—on your personal balance sheet—implementing economic scarcity within your business will lead to a better company. Not a scarcity mentality, mind you, just a healthy tension between resources and objectives. An organization that feels like it has all the money in the world to throw at a problem will only seek to solve problems by throwing money at them.

For example, several of the most highly funded film budgets have produced some of the biggest flops in Hollywood history. Have you ever heard of *Heaven's Gate*, starring Kris Kristofferson? No big surprise if you haven't; it was a colossal failure at the box office because audiences found it long and boring. It was also one of the biggest-budget films of the early 1980s, making it a large contributing factor to the ensuing shutdown of its studio, United Artists.

In his talks, Alan Chaffee cites a number of times where companies that have engaged his outsourced CFO services made better, more innovative decisions because they weren't swimming in a sea of available capital. By remaining lean, these companies had to come up with incredible solutions—which eventually led to greater profits—instead of falling for the temptation of just throwing money at their problems. The biggest problem Alan notices after his clients have implemented his strategies to create more profit in their businesses is that they also tend to increase their personal spending!

It is common in our culture to talk about saving for the future, and while that is important, we make a distinction between savings and building assets. When speaking to a large room, we will often ask the question, "What is it most people eventually do with savings?" and we always get the same answer: "Spend it!" The reason is that the cultural mindset around savings has built up with spending at the core. Don't we usually talk about "saving up" for something? It is not clear when the idea of saving actually turned into eventual spending, so rather than fighting our country's cultural definition of savings, we defined a completely different area of conversation.

Everyone still needs short-term save-to-spend kinds of accounts. Home maintenance, health care, vacations, Christmas gifts, or a general emergency fund are all examples of short-term savings accounts we have seen clients build up. We suggest clients start at six months of personal spending in cash and overtime work toward one year of expenses in cash or near-term liquid assets. We call this your emergency fund. For money that is meant to buy assets and grow for the long term, we need a separate account: a Wealth Coordination Account.

Paul first introduced the idea of a Wealth Coordination Account (WCA) in the opening episode of our weekly show, also titled *Your Business Your Wealth*. If you have been reading straight through, you will remember that we outlined this concept at greater length in chapter 3, but for those who are jumping around, this refers to a separate checking account where you keep extra money that you intend to use to purchase assets.

When we talk to our clients about WCAs, most ask why they can't just use a savings account or an IRA. Financial institutions would surely prefer that you simply add money on a consistent monthly basis, right out of your household checking, to the products they sell you. With the WCA, though, we want you to have an account that you can use, by design, to buy assets. This account will allow you to accumulate money for your asset building and then periodically deploy it, allowing *you* to drive your own wealth-building action.

What distinguishes a Wealth Coordination Account from a normal checking account is its one and only purpose: it exists solely for creating Definite Financial Independence, where you no longer rely on your business to support your lifestyle. Another extremely important point about a Wealth Coordination Account is that it's the first bill you pay every month. It's the first line item on your budget, too. You can have other goals you choose to put money toward, but none of them cuts the line in front of your Wealth Coordination Account.

By putting money in a completely separate account—one for buying assets—you will be far less tempted to use it for any other reason. You should never use a WCA the way you would use a traditional savings account, such as for a car repair or a vacation home purchase. Those are lifestyle purchases, not asset investments. The benefit of separating lifestyle spending in your household checking/savings, and asset building in your WCA, is that it is hard to accidentally spend money that isn't there. If you first separate money into your WCA to handle your future, you now have the freedom to say, "Whatever I still have in savings, I'll buy what I want with it."

How do you start creating this incredible personal-wealth-building tool? Again, you make it the first bill you pay every month. Take at least 20% of your income and a percentage of your company's profit and put it in that Wealth Coordination Account before you spend the money on anything else. The other way to build your Wealth Coordination Account is through the sale of any assets you previously purchased. This way, the dollars you have planted for the future are able to continue to compound for you until you choose to lean on them instead of your business to fund your lifestyle.

It's Not What You Make; It's What You Keep

The math behind reaching Definite Financial Independence is simple. The insights we often share come from a blogger named Peter Adeney, better known by his pseudonym and website title, *Mr. Money Mustache.*

Despite the funny name, Mr. Money Mustache's insights into saving money have been featured on *CBS News, MarketWatch,* and the *New Yorker,* among others. The man lives radically within his own means, spending far less than the $400,000 a year he now makes from his blog. Back in 2012, he exploded in popularity after writing a blog post entitled, "The Shockingly Simple Math Behind Early Retirement." His point was that early retirement only depends on the *percentage* of your income that you save. The higher you can increase that amount, the earlier you can retire.

SAVINGS RATE (PERCENT)	WORKNG YEARS UNTIL RETIREMENT
5	66
10	51
15	43
20	37
25	32
30	28
35	25
40	22
45	19
50	17
55	14.5
60	12.5
65	10.5
70	8.5
75	7
80	5.5
85	4
90	Under 3
95	Under 2
100	Zero

Here is what Mr. Money Mustache is getting at: the higher your savings rate grows as a percentage of income, the lower your lifestyle becomes relative to your income. That means that your assets have a lower income number they need to generate. In his chart, he points to an 85% savings rate leading to independence in only 4 years.

	INCOME	$300,000.00
	SAVINGS RATE	85.00%
	ROR	5.00%
	LIFESTYLE	$45,000.00
	ASSETS	**INCOME AT 4%**
YEAR 1	$267,750.00	$10,710.00
YEAR 2	$548,887.50	$21,955.50
YEAR 3	$844,081.88	$33,763.28
YEAR 4	$1,154,035.97	$46,161.44

If a household enjoyed $300,000 of income and could save 85% of it, that means they were living their life with only $45,000 of spending each year. At a 5% rate of return (Peter's assumption), that savings rate would produce an asset level big enough to fund that lifestyle (Peter is using the 4% rule, too!) in only 4 years.

Most people think that it's the amount they make that will decide when they can call it quits. If that were true, though, most of us making high six figures would be living that nothing-but-weekends lifestyle by now. Like Jeff's grandfather told us earlier, it's not the amount of income you make. It's the amount you keep on your personal balance sheet that matters.

Determining what you need to be content—as in the sufficiency, surplus, and superfluence exercise from chapter 3—is the easiest way to decide how much money to set aside. The more content you are, the less you need, and the more you can take out of each paycheck to put toward building your personal balance sheet. You also have far less to replace in terms of the income you need to continue living your lifestyle after your business is gone. You're not just saving more; you're actually pulling the finish line toward you by becoming more content. We know what you were probably thinking while reading the Mr. Money Mustache example: something like "Save 85%? I live off of 85%!" The Mustache family made some very radical decisions about changing their lifestyle, and we know that won't work for everyone. But everybody has the ability to move that needle over time, especially business owners. Even if you are setting aside a relatively low percentage of your income now, you can create dramatic new results by *not spending more as you increase your income.*

According to Peter's chart, if you made $150,000 per year and saved 10%, you would need 51 years of work to be able to retire. If you are able to double your business and increase your income to $300,000, but you also double your lifestyle and still only save 10%, then you don't change your trajectory on the 51-year course.

If instead you saved 50% of your new $300,000 income, you would have chopped that 51-year timeline down to 17 years. Contentment doesn't have to be about settling for less; it can also mean realizing you are okay not chasing *more.* And by the way, this example still took the family from a $135,000 lifestyle to a $150,000 lifestyle. You can keep giving more to your family year after year, just ask yourself: Which do I want to grow faster, my present or my future?

While the math is simple, the required behaviors are not. Remember Odysseus. He understood the threats posed by the Sirens, and he knew he had to put systems in place to survive: insert beeswax, tie rope to the mast, and instruct his men to not let him free under any circumstance.

That's why we recommend making the 20% contribution to your Wealth Coordination Account automatic. It's a simple system that won't challenge your self-discipline every month. And as you continue to culti-vate contentment, you may find yourself looking for ways to increase that percentage, using these systems to maximize your speed toward Definite Financial Independence.

If you would like help building these calculations for yourself, follow this link to calculators on our site: _YBYWbook.com_

How Much Would Your Family Need Without You?

Before we move on, here's one more way to think about how much you need on your personal balance sheet. If you're making $600,000 a year, that's the amount your whole family has become accustomed to living on as well, even if they don't know how much you are creating for them. Presumably, you're not spending all of that money on yourself. It's going toward the mortgage (maybe more than one), car payments, school tuition, utilities, groceries, and other living expenses (and hopefully setting some money aside for the future).

While it's not fun to think about, if something were to happen to you and you were no longer around to be that source of human capital, how would your family make up for that loss of income? As macabre as that situation is, it is the same reality from a cash-flow standpoint as if you sold your business or decided to stop working.

As odd as it might seem, the answer to the question "How much life insurance do I want?" should be a number remarkably close to the answer to "How much money do I need to build Definite Financial Independence to fund my work-optional lifestyle?"

Does that seem like an odd way to look at life insurance? If your homeowners insurance provides enough coverage to fully replace your home if it burned down, and your auto insurance would replace your car if it was totaled, then is there any reason why you wouldn't have enough life insurance to replace the value of the income you are expected to earn over the rest of your career?

If you are over the age of 30, one reason is that you'll have a very hard time finding a policy that replaces your total salary. Insurance companies are not willing to over-insure anyone, because that leads to people behaving badly. Just like an auto insurance company could anticipate that someone might wreck their Honda Civic the day after they bought a $1 million policy on it, life insurance companies don't want spouses to start doing math in the middle of a fight. Both of our wives know that we are worth much more alive than not, even though we both have put in place the maximum amount of life insurance that the industry would allow us to have.

This is just one more reason why you want to build a robust personal balance sheet next to your business. Someday you and your family may depend on it.

Chapter 5:
Money Mechanics and Financial Illusions

ONE REASON MANY OF OUR CLIENTS SEEK OUR HELP IS HOW BUSY THEY are. They just don't have the time to get all the information they need to make the decisions they must.

That's why we wrote this book. We want to distill the most important information business owners need to create fulfilling financial lives and put it all in one easily accessible place.

However, another reason people struggle with managing their money—or choosing the right people to do it for them—is how much misinformation is out there. We completely understand how highly intelligent people can make costly mistakes with their hard-earned money. Personal finance is a minefield for those who are unfamiliar with the terrain.

In this chapter, we are going to give you some prime examples that prove just how perilous personal finance can be.

Survival of the (Financial) Fittest

If you ask most people where the exact turning point was that led to an Allied victory in World War II, you'll probably hear answers like Hiroshima or Nagasaki, the Battle of the Bulge, or D-Day.

Those all have their merits and we certainly don't want to take anything away from the brave men and women who sacrificed themselves in those battles, but we do want to introduce you to another very important hero who doesn't get nearly enough credit.

To us, the turning point of World War II may have occurred in a smoke-filled apartment in Harlem, New York City. There, a group of brainy mathematicians working for the US government was tasked with analyzing field data sent back from Allied generals. The hope was that a statistician's mind might be able to harvest new insights that could help win the war.

In practice, the plan almost led to the Allies' defeat.

At one point these mathematicians were studying the scatter graphs of returning aircraft, which showed where they had been hit by enemy fire.

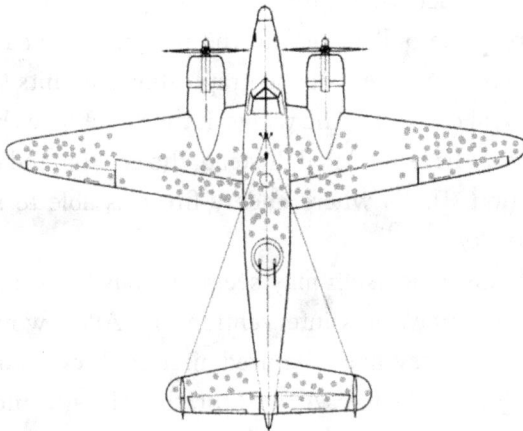

The statisticians were entrusted with finding out where the best places would be to add more armor and how much less in fuel and munitions the planes would be able to carry as a result.

It was extremely important work, because the Allies had a distinct advantage over the Nazis in airpower. In fact, many experts think that a Nazi victory could have happened if the Luftwaffe had developed long-range bombing capabilities. In other words, the Allies really needed to keep this advantage and press it for every gain possible. Therefore, these researchers figured out the right balance between more armor and less range. The planes would have less bombing capacity and less effective range, but fewer would get shot down. At least, that's what this team thought.

Fortunately, a man by the name of Abraham Wald interceded just as the results of their calculations were headed out the door. He pointed out that the entire approach to the problem was misguided. The planes that made it back weren't good references for how to keep them from getting shot out of the sky. Clearly, those planes had delivered their deadly payload and made it back to the airfield. In fact it was a rare event that a plane came back from a mission without bullet holes. Instead, Wald advised, they needed to understand what happened with the planes that *didn't* make it back.

Take another look at that scatter graph. The team of analysts thought more armor was needed where the bullets were hitting. Wald knew the opposite was true. The bullet holes in the pictures didn't represent a fatality for the mission. Notice that the graph shows no hits to the cockpit, engines, or the weakest part of the wings. If the bullet holes had been fatal, the planes wouldn't have returned. Instead, the cockpit and engines needed more protection. That's where enemy fire was able to snatch Allied planes out of the sky.

Even though this conclusion may seem obvious to us now, it was not obvious then. Without Wald's intervention, the Allies would have completely changed how they manufactured aircraft. They would have been no safer and a lot less effective. As a result, the Allies would have all but discarded one of their greatest advantages.

Don't Just Look at the Survivors

Wald became famous among his peers for using the theory of survivorship bias. In entrepreneurship, anyone who succeeds is considered a survivor.

Recall those statistics we mentioned in chapter 1. For every entrepreneur who can start a business and keep it in operation for 10 years, 8 to 10 others fail. For every business owner who succeeds at creating more than $1 million in revenues, 40 do not. Yet, the vast majority of financial advice out there for business owners is based solely on the survivors, especially those who defied the odds of creating $1 million in revenue. Those are the entrepreneurs who get studied and the ones whom others look to for advice. It's survivorship bias in action.

Of course there is lots to learn from entrepreneurs who succeed. Every business book (including this one!) looks to past successes for insights, as do magazines such as *Inc.* or podcasts like Tim Ferriss's. But we also need to look at the whole range of the continuum. If we don't study those who fail, know why people fail, we can't fully understand why other entrepreneurs succeed.

For example, let's say that 80% of all successful entrepreneurs don't pay themselves a salary for the first five years. Most "experts" out there would take that information and tell their clients to do the same. After all, the majority of successful entrepreneurs do this.

However, a closer look at the facts might show you that 90% of entrepreneurs who fail don't pay themselves a salary for the first five years, either. In light of that, it seems as though the 80% who succeed do so in spite of that habit.

Here's another reason why entrepreneurs need to be very careful about whom they look to for advice.

Inevitably, when we bring up the dangers of survivorship bias, someone will retort with a story about an entrepreneur they know who made it. They had, say, a $4 million sale and now they're living the good life. This person isn't worried about survivorship bias, because they know a survivor and will just follow their lead.

The great danger here is that some entrepreneurs may look as though they made it when, in reality, they're just barely getting by. For example, one of our clients was a former business owner who did this very thing. This man had earned a very impressive $40-million exit in the late 1990s, but not long into our first conversation, we learned that he and his wife had never quit living their superfluent lifestyle after the big payday. They had never sat down and determined how to live sufficiently.

By the time we met, they had $2.5 million left and they were still spending it fast, distributing over $300,000 a year from their investments. When we brought up that they would likely run out of money, he said that his current advisor, whom he had used for years, thought the market would continue to support his lifestyle. After creating a new relationship and laying out the danger he and his wife were in over the coming decade, he chose to simply stay with his current strategy and risk running out.

Of course, to everyone else, it looked as though they had taken their $40 million and wisely invested it. They owned more than one gigantic home. They also had multiple supercars and collectible cars aside from the ones they regularly drove. Even their kids had more expensive vehicles than almost any adult we knew.

Those who didn't know any better thought he was the man to follow. And his judgment was clouded because he had an advisor telling him what he wanted to hear.

Again, there are plenty of successful entrepreneurs worth modeling yourself after. The point is that between survivorship bias and illusory success stories, you need to be careful who you choose.

Mastering the Market (Just Like Everyone Else)

Studying survivorship bias shows all the more reason to build your personal balance sheet instead of hoping for a legendary exit.

But where do you put the money to work? Over the years, a lot of people have asked us why they can't just look up a few highly rated mutual funds and invest there. It seems like a lot less work. You just continue adding more to the fund every year and stand to enjoy modest but dependable returns without much in the way of risk. While no mutual fund manager would ever guarantee that their fund can beat the market, most go a long way toward alluding to those results.

Low risk and better-than-market results? Who in their right mind wouldn't take advantage of a mutual fund?

While we have seen mutual funds that have beaten the market, no one has ever been able to find a fund that can do so consistently.

In fact, research shows that over a 20-year period, only about 23% of mutual funds ever beat the indexes they are being compared to.[1]

---

1   Analysis performed by Dimensional Fund Advisors. Beginning sample includes US-domiciled funds as of the beginning of the 20-year period ending Devember 31, 2018. The number of beginners is indicated below the asset class

THEY TRY TO PICK WINNERS...

FRACTION OF MUTUAL FUNDS THAT BEAT THEIR BENCHMARK FOR 20 YEARS, ENDING DECEMBER 31, 2018

STOCKS
2,414 BEGINNING

`23%`

BONDS
1,826 BEGINNING

`8%`

Analysis performed by Dimensional Fund Advisors. Beginning sample includes US-domiciled funds as of the beginning of the 20-year period ending December 31, 2018. The number of beginners is indicated below the asset class label. Outperformers (winners) are funds that had returns for every month in the sample period and outperformed their benchmark over the period. US-domiciled mutual fund data is provided by Morningstar. See Data Appendix for more information. Past performance is no guarantee of future results.

That's not a very promising statistic. It's even worse when you consider that only 34.11% of large-cap mutual funds existed for 15 years before their sponsoring financial institutions shut them down. [find source information at _YWBWbook.com_].

Once again, survivorship bias rears its ugly head.

This kind of bias can be at play on a much smaller scale, too. Have you ever been to a party or some function where someone's holding court by talking about the three stocks they bought last year that gave them a 100% rate of return? You know the type.

Maybe he's telling the truth. Maybe he's experiencing a false or incomplete memory, as all of us do from time to time. Or maybe he's only telling part of the truth—only referencing the survivors.

What we all tend to leave out when recounting our stories are the failures that were a net negative on our net worth. We've also noticed that just how much these people actually invest tends to be left out of the story, too. Perhaps the guy really did buy Apple stock back when it was only $20 a share, but he fails to mention that he only bought $200 worth.

---

label. Outperformers (winners) are funds that had returns for every month in the sample period and outperformed their benchmark over the period. US-domiciled mutual fund data is provided by Morningstar. See Data Appendix for more information. Past performance is no guarantee of future results.

The active management of stock portfolios is always an attractive story. It is attractive, however, because it is almost always a fantasy. "Beating the market" is never our goal. All the academic evidence out there shows us that professional stock pickers can't actually beat the market in any predictable fashion, either. We seek to help clients experience the rate of return of the market as efficiently as possible, cutting out excess cost and inefficiency in their portfolios. (More on this in chapter 6.)

Planning for Other People's Life Expectancies

We cannot discuss retirement planning without talking about life expectancy. It's definitely not the most pleasant topic, but we have to plan for how long you'll need money after you quit earning a regular income. Your resources need to last from the day you retire until the last day you breathe.

Unfortunately, life expectancy is another area where misunderstandings run wild. Even though it is absolutely essential in order to plan for retirement, the way most people think about it—including many financial advisors—is so fraught with error that it dooms the entire process from the very beginning.

How long does the average person live? Whenever we ask people this question, we get a range of answers, but they tend to hover right around 78.6 or so. In fact that is the exact number you get if you Google "life expectancy in the US." That's because newspapers, magazines, and online articles constantly print stories about how long the average baby boomer, man or woman, lives.

The problem with these numbers is twofold. First, life expectancy is a 50/50 statistic! If 78 is the median life expectancy for baby boomers, that just means one half of that demographic will have passed away by 78, and the other half will live some amount longer. No life expectancy number you find should be the end point of your planning; it is merely the fuzzy midpoint.

Second, national life expectancy numbers, even for a specific demographic like baby boomers, are still national averages that leave too many variables off the table. Our country has large disparities in health depending on where someone lives, how much education they have, and how easy it is to access health care and good nutrition. A lot of that has to do with economic disparity. As a nation we definitely have some work to do in those areas, which is a topic for another book, but the fact remains for now that just by virtue of being at the level of income and business success you have reached, you are probably *above average* in access to health care and access to information on how to eat well, exercise, and in general live in a way that extends your life. If we start narrowing down the demographic to more narrowly match your metrics, that 78-year life expectancy will start moving up fast.

The question you want to answer is, "What is your life expectancy based on your specific situation?" If you shoot for an average like 78, remember that by the very nature of that number, half of you are going to live longer—perhaps a lot longer. Imagine reaching 78, with a likely road of 10 to 20 years still in front of you, and realizing that you had reached the edge of your map in planning for your financial future.

AGE 65 AND HEALTHY... LIVE TO AGE 93

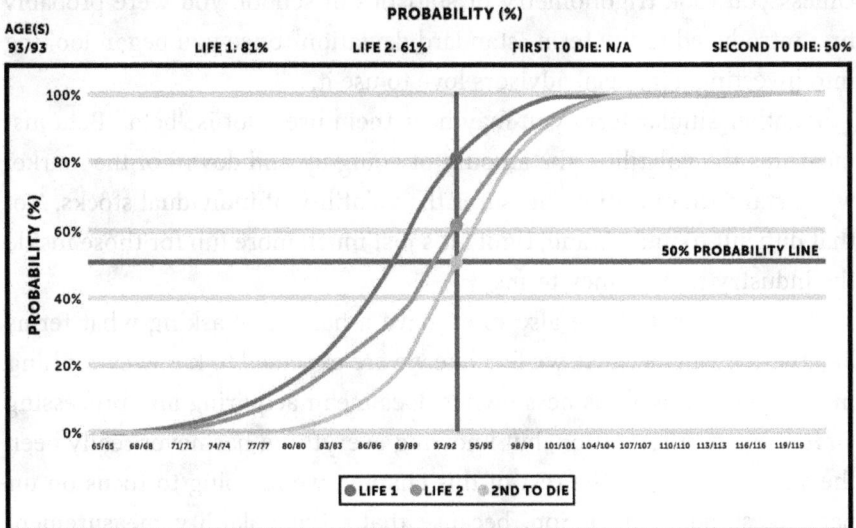

AGE(S) 93/93   **PROBABILITY (%)**

LIFE 1: 81%   LIFE 2: 61%   FIRST TO DIE: N/A   SECOND TO DIE: 50%

The national average life expectancy numbers are no more useful to you than basing your planning on other people's heights and weights. It makes absolutely no sense.

If you are married, the only other person whose life expectancy should be factored into your retirement planning is your spouse's. Your joint life expectancy is the average age at which the second of the two of you will pass away. You need to think about joint life expectancy because one of you is going to outlive the other, and the capital at work that you have set aside needs to last at least until then. Furthermore, married couples tend to live longer—much longer—on average than individuals. The red line in the chart below is from life insurance industry data, and that industry has a vested interest in understanding these numbers. Long after 78, a married couple's age of mortality is all the way up at 93. Again, that's just the median. For 50% of couples, one of them will live some span past 93!

That means, for a lot of us, the money we set aside while we are working will have to last longer than the total years we worked!

What Is Risk? Standard Deviation Explained

Unless you took trigonometry or statistics in school, you were probably first introduced to the term "standard deviation" once you began looking into investing. Financial advisors love to use it.

Another similar term you may hear them use a lot is "beta." Beta just measures the volatility (the amount of going up and down) of the market while standard deviation measures the volatility of individual stocks. Not that difficult to understand, right? It's just much more fun for those inside the industry to use fancy terms.

As entrepreneurs, we also often have a hard time asking what terms like these mean, because we feel like we are expected to know everything. In fairness, being a business owner does mean acquiring and processing large sums of information, but knowing everything has never really been the standard. So, for the rest of this chapter, we're going to focus on unpacking standard deviation, because that's the volatility measurement applied to most investment portfolios.

8% RATE OF RETURN EVERY YEAR

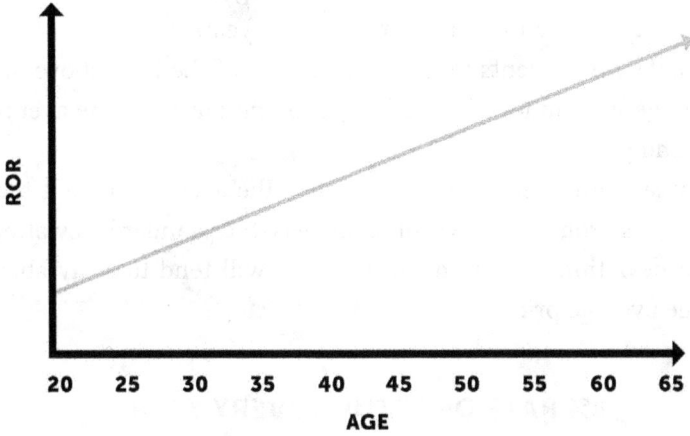

The chart below shows an 8% rate of return every year. As you can see, in this scenario, it's smooth, up, and to the right the entire time. This would be an *ideal* situation for investments.

This total lack of volatility would be nice, but it doesn't work that way. That stock is going to increase and decrease in price over time. It may trend higher, but it will perform above and below its "average return" along the way.

8% RATE OF RETURN EVERY YEAR

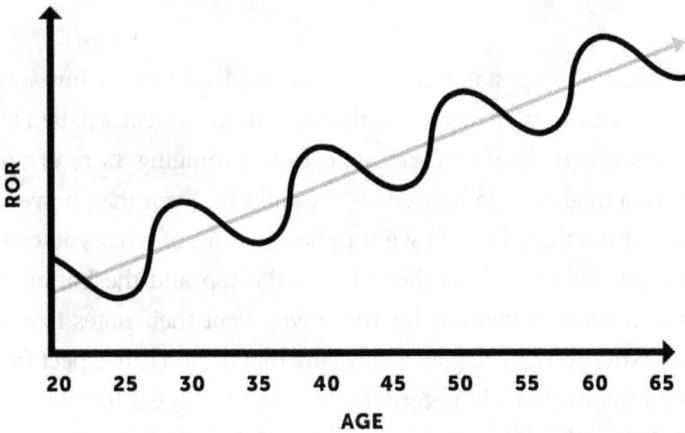

Many individual investors relate to "average return" as what they can expect to experience in their portfolio most years, but as you can see in the example, investments tend to spend most of the time above or below that average line, and we only ever get to find out what the average *was* months and years later.

If that smooth line is the average, then the average amount the stock ever deviates from it—above or below—is the standard deviation. The standard deviation is how much the price will tend to stray above and below the average price.

8% RATE OF RETURN EVERY YEAR

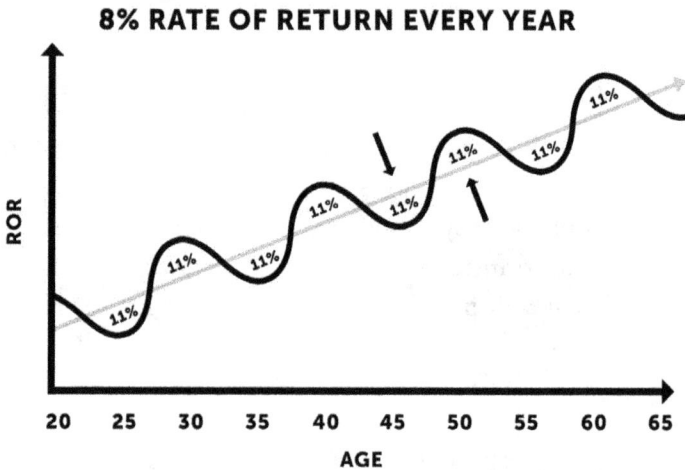

Your portfolio has a standard deviation, too, based on its investments. If you have an 11% standard deviation, then 68% of the time it will be 11% *above or below* the average. So if you have a portfolio averaging 8% return per year, your portfolio might range between +19% and -3%. Even that, however, only covers 68% of the time. Do you want to be 95% sure of what you can expect from your portfolio? Add another 11% on the top and the bottom (that is called two standard deviations for those who kept their notes from college stats class). Now you can be reasonably sure that *all* you can expect from your portfolio on the way to a long-term 8% average is to see it fluctuate between +30% and -14% in the days, weeks, months, and years in between.

8% RATE OF RETURN EVERY YEAR

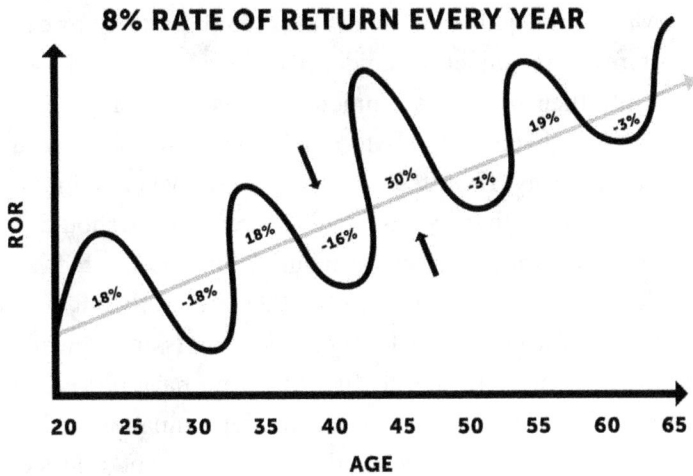

This is what risk really means: accepting a wider range of potential outcomes in your strategy. An FDIC-backed certificate of deposit has 0% standard deviation in the outcome, because the rate of return is set in advance, and guaranteed by a contract between the bank and the FDIC in case the bank was to fail.

Risk Tolerance vs. Loss Tolerance

You can't talk to a financial advisor for more than two minutes without hearing the term "risk tolerance." Early on, every client learns that the returns they can expect to see will depend on the amount of risk they're going to take. When you look at it from that angle, it becomes pretty easy to take on more risk. You want higher returns, right? It almost sounds like the cool kid in the schoolyard leaving you under the impression that you are not cool if you don't do something risky. It's the "no pain, no gain" of the financial world.

Of course, people who believe they need to push through pain to gain generally end up in a lot of pain with nothing to show for it. The same tends to be true with risky investing. When someone says they're willing to take on more risk, what we hear them saying is, "In order to reach my personal balance sheet goals, I am willing to accept a greater probability of completely missing them entirely."

That doesn't sound quite as harmless as accepting a little more risk, does it? Yet, most investors—under the guidance of their financial advisors—keep adding risk into their portfolios. Numerous advisors and big-box financial firms even give their clients tests to assess their risk tolerance in an extremely superficial way. These tests are like the ones you find in the back of *Cosmopolitan* magazine that promise to tell you whom you should date once your score is tallied. They are about as nuanced and reliable, too.

One main issue with these tests is that they are subtly but surely pushing consumers toward a greater level of risk. Clients are typically scored on a risk scale that goes from 0 to 100. At 0, you have no risk tolerance and, presumably, at 100, you have the grim determination and keen eye of a fighter pilot, willing to risk anything at a moment's notice for the greater good.

We've been trained by years of schooling to want to get A's on our tests, or score 100, so investors subconsciously answer questions in ways that will bring their score closer and closer to 100—the high-risk end of the spectrum. Therefore, the average investor is likely to end up with a higher score and, thus, a higher "tolerance" for risk.

Rather than "risk tolerance," think instead in terms of your loss tolerance: How much can you lose and still afford to hold your portfolio's overall strategy? Thinking about "risk tolerance" tends to have us focus on the payoff we hope to receive for taking that risk, and we have no problem "tolerating" the thought of a big win. But then we are unprepared for the potential downsides that come with that risk. Investors in this position are not expecting the downturns that eventually come in the world of investing. The shock usually causes them to change their strategy, either selling out of the investment and making the loss permanent, or increasing the risk to chase higher returns and recover their losses.

Risk doesn't need to be treated like one of the more taboo four-letter words, but it's also extremely dangerous to play with when you don't know how much you can tolerate losing before you start feeling like you chose the wrong strategy. What really makes this such an insidious threat is that additional risk can often pay off in the short term. Before the real estate market bubble burst in the mid-2000s, a lot of people put more money into both the stock market and the real estate market. Both markets looked to be on an unstoppable upward trajectory, so a lot of people—under the guidance of "more risk is required for more returns"—broke from their previous strategy (if they had one) to chase their fortunes.

When the markets fell in one of the steepest declines since the Great Depression, lots of investors felt they had miscalculated. But the biggest mistakes of the 2008 financial crisis were not made in the days of the steepest market drops in that year. The biggest mistakes were made several years before, the moment investors started chasing promises of greater gain with no thought about their loss tolerance.

Don't Fall for Tempting Untruths

Just as alluring as the Sirens' song, the illusions we covered above often represent similar temptations. It's easy to accept that "more risk equals more reward" during a bull market. It's easy to ignore terms like "standard deviation" when it seems like your financial advisor has everything under control. We would all like to follow successful survivors down the path of chart-busting returns. Of course, this isn't how disciplined investing works. Successful investing takes planning and the right systems in place around your balance sheet.

In the next chapter, we're going to continue to explore loss tolerance and learn how discovering your personal loss tolerance can help avoid temptations the marketplace will throw at you.

Chapter 6:
The Only Way to Beat the Market

IN THE PREVIOUS CHAPTER, WE BRIEFLY TOUCHED ON HOW NO ONE CAN actually beat the market—at least not reliably and consistently over time.

In this chapter, we're going to delve deeper into that point, because despite the fact that there is unquestionable research that proves there is no predictability to when or how active managers beat the market from time to time, many investors still line up to hand over their hard-earned money to "experts" who say otherwise. We're going to talk about why these untruths aren't going anywhere and ensure you understand the only way people are ever able to actually beat the market.

However, it's also important to understand why we are devoting so much space to this topic. It's because of the "risk tolerance versus loss tolerance" distinction we made in the last chapter and how often people deviate from their strategy because they don't understand the difference. This distinction is the reason that leads so many investors to abandon their strategy, making short-term moves that eventually destroy their financial future.

Let's begin by looking at the most common reason people believe they can do better than the market on a consistent basis.

Mutual Funds: "Masters" of the Market

As you'll recall from chapter 5, mutual funds are pitched as the most reasonable investment you could ever make. Sure, bonds are extremely reliable, and some individual stocks may even earn the same description. However, most financial advisors will tell you that there is no safer, better bet than a mutual fund.

I know what you are thinking: surely it has *nothing* to do with the fact that they're the ones who are actually selling them.[2]

Nearly the entire mutual fund industry is based on the biggest myth in all of investing, which, again, is that someone can predictably outsmart the market over time. This is the one and only message most mutual fund managers offer in order to win clients and keep them:

"Invest your money with us. We're the *only* smart people who can beat the market."

That's not to say there aren't some other tantalizing bells and whistles added to the cart, too. For example, the company will offer to take care of nearly everything for you. You don't even need to watch the market. Just send them your money and they'll keep "beating the market" with it, "a set it and forget it" strategy. Best of all, it's only going to cost you 1% to 1.5% per year.

What is particularly powerful about this "beat-the-market" myth is that it's propped up by almost the entire investing industry. After all, no matter how badly one firm wants to beat another, they can't very well announce, "Look, none of us can actually beat the market, but we promise to lose to it by the very least." Even the opposing sides of the industry are actually telling the same tale.

On one side of the financial industry, we have the advisory firms, selling mutual funds with the mantra "We can beat the market." The biggest competitor to that business, sitting across the table competing for your dollars, are all the online trading platforms that have sprung up since 2000.

These companies don't tell you, "*We* can beat the market." With their technology leading the way, the major innovation they've brought to investing is to tell the individual investor, "*You* can beat the market." Of course, that means you need to open an account with them, but that's positioned as being far better than giving your money to those mutual funds.

---

2   It may actually have something to do with who is selling them.

Unfortunately, it's all one big false premise, the biggest myth we cover in the book, with Odysseus's tale coming in a distant second. While the traditional advisory business and online trading platforms are competing for customers with financial magazine and television ads like some drunken street brawl, they are both pushing the exact same narrative: *someone* can consistently and predictably beat market returns. They just disagree as to whether that person is you or your advisor.

We could fill an entire book with all the studies that prove you can't consistently beat the market, but here's just one more example: if you look at the University of Chicago's research from their Center for Research in Security Prices, Morningstar investment study, you'll see for yourself that mutual funds don't tackle markets quite as well as their managers would lead you to believe.

Morningstar, which may be the most well-known and respected mutual fund research firm, uses a five-star system to rank funds based on risk-adjusted returns. A five-star fund is best, and one-star is the worst. But how do five-star funds actually *perform* compared to their lower-ranked competitors? When you look at how five-star funds perform over time,

Is There Predictive Power in Morningstar Ratings?

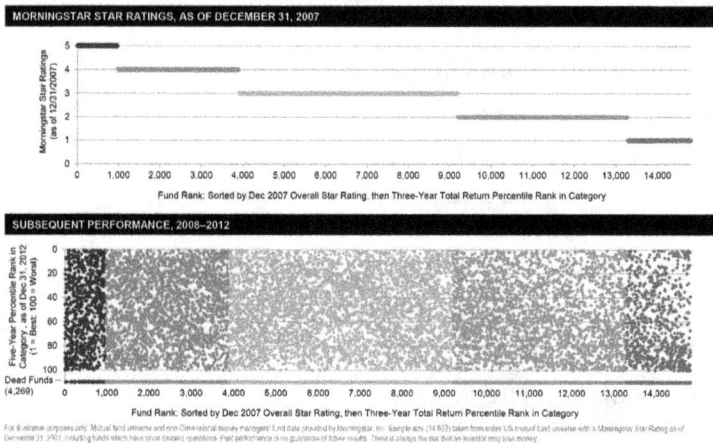

Source: Dimensional Fund Advisors

you find absolutely no correlation whatsoever with an equally impressive performance. The designation may as well be completely arbitrary.

In fact, the same goes for four-star funds, which are also considered top performers. You see the same with two- and three-star funds. There's just no historical data that justifies predicting one will do any better than the others.

Interestingly, the one-star funds are where you have any chance whatsoever of predictability, as they clump together as the poorest performers in the time frame tracked above. Though in reality, all that allows you to do is avoid those funds, not make good investment decisions that could outperform the market. Some—definitely not the majority—may eventually become five-star funds. Remember, though, there's just no way to predict this kind of performance.

How Pattern Recognition Can Lead to Bad Investment Decisions

So, what's going on here? Why are so many people falling for this ploy, especially when it means putting their financial futures at risk? There are a few reasons.

One is good old-fashioned wishful thinking. Of course, we all want to believe that something as simple as a mutual fund could actually work. It would be great if we could just send 20% of every paycheck to an expert investor and they would make sure it returned better than the market year after year—and at such an affordable price.

Now, to be fair, a second reason is that these funds spend such large sums on convincing us that this is true. There is no lack of marketing where your money's future is concerned, and most of it is coming from mutual funds.

Third, with so many people doing it, how could it possibly be a bad idea? It's not like mutual funds are new. Literally millions of people have invested in them since they were first introduced almost a century ago. It can be very difficult to accept that so many people are using the wrong strategy.

Finally, the most fundamental reason is pattern recognition. As humans, we're predisposed to—and are exceptionally good at—finding patterns in all things. Doing so promoted a higher level of human survival early in our history. For example, if you had never seen them before, it probably wouldn't take you long to realize that dark clouds mean it's likely to rain soon, and you should seek shelter if you want to stay dry.

At the same time, we often find patterns where they don't exist. This explains many superstitions, like athletes who won't wash their socks when they're on a winning streak. Or maybe you know that you're going to have a bad day at work when the line at Starbucks is too long, because the two have coincided a few times before. Rationally, we know that what we're witnessing is a correlation, not causation. Nonetheless, our pattern-happy brains can't help but make a case for this illusion.

When we speak at conferences, we provide a simple example of pattern recognition gone awry. We put out one $1 US coin for each person at every table, and we instruct the attendees to pick up their coin and stand. After everyone is at attention, we let them know that they are all new active managers for a large mutual fund company. The mutual fund company has given them each $10 million to manage, represented by the coin they now possess.

Because each asset manager has about a 50% chance of beating the market each year, and there is no way to predict which manager will do so on a year-to-year basis, the coin is a great metaphor for active management. Each time the coin is flipped, if they land on heads they stay in the game. If they land on tails, they are "fired," and they have to sit down and hand all their money under management (their coin) to a person left standing. That is what can (and does) happen at a large fund company—when your performance as a new manager lags, they simply roll the assets into another one of the incubator funds, and you join that team or find a new job.

After five flips, the crowd has winnowed and those left standing are now considered "experts" at managing money. When we ask about their technique, the "expert" flippers will usually offer some sincere tips on style. Whatever their secret technique is, the truth is that if you flip a coin enough times, eventually you're going to get five heads or five tails in a row. If you have a ballroom full of people flip a coin five times, someone is bound to have the same result just through blind luck.

The exact same degree of chance is alive and well in the market. How well active mutual funds do over long periods of time is almost *completely* random. Yet, it's human nature to look for the pattern. We innately seek predictable behavior because, well, that's a lot more comforting than the alternative. Wouldn't you feel a lot better "knowing" that one mutual fund outperforms everyone else because the manager has decades of experience, rather than finding out that it was more akin to the flip of a coin?

Despite the overwhelming academic evidence, many investors are slow to embrace this point.

We encounter this type of optimism in other financial sectors, too. Real estate is a prime example. By the end of 2002, it seemed like the whole world had become "expert" real estate investors, and those who weren't in the game grew more tempted each year. Confidence was flying high in 2004, 2005, 2006, and even in 2007.

Then, 2008 and 2009 came. *That's* when we found out who the real experts were. Turns out there weren't very many. These scenarios play out over and over, sometimes in relatively quick succession, and the vast majority of investors seem not to want to learn this *helpful* pattern.

Before the real estate bubble, it was the tech bubble. You may remember, during the late 1990s, reading profiles of highly paid professionals, top performers in their fields, who quit their jobs to day-trade stocks. Dentists shut down their practices to stay home and day-trade tech stocks. Over a short period of time, there were fewer and fewer surviving "winners," just like in our coin-flipping demonstration. Some people managed to escape with only nominal losses, but many ended up losing nearly their entire net worth. It is easy to forget just how bad that period was for investors, as well as how quickly most of us were willing to jump into the next sure thing.

How to Create a "Winning" Fund

Despite the academic evidence, actively managed mutual funds continue to find eager investors. One way is by creating what *appears* to be a fund that does nothing but win. It's effective and entirely legal, but it is trickery. Understanding this will change the way you view actively managed funds forever. Most asset managers don't even beat the index they're being compared to for 5 years, much less 10. You can find some that do, but their odds of success continue to decrease over time—just like your ability to continue flipping a quarter and getting the same side many times in a row. The following chart summarizes a study that asks a simple question: How often do top-performing funds repeat their results? The study selects a series of 5-year periods, and identifies which mutual funds were the top 25% of all performers for that 5-year period. Then the study tracks how those all-stars did over the next 5 years. On average, 79% of the former high performers fail to repeat their performance in the top 25%.

Past Performance Is Not Enough to Predict Future Results

Percentage of US-based funds that were top-quartile performers in consecutive five-year periods

PAST PERFORMANCE IS NOT ENOUGH TO PREDICT FUTURE RESULTS

PERCENTAGE OF US-BASED FUNDS THAT WERE TOP-QUARTILE PERFORMERS IN CONSECUTIVE FIVE-YEAR PERIODS

EQUITY FUNDS

Period	Following 5 Years
2004-2008	28%
2005-2009	23%
2006-2010	23%
2007-2011	19%
2008-2012	16%
2009-2013	14%
2010-2014	19%
2011-2015	22%
2012-2016	21%
2013-2017	23%
2014-2018	25%

PREVIOUS 5 YEARS	FOLLOWING 5 YEARS	21% AVERAGE	100%

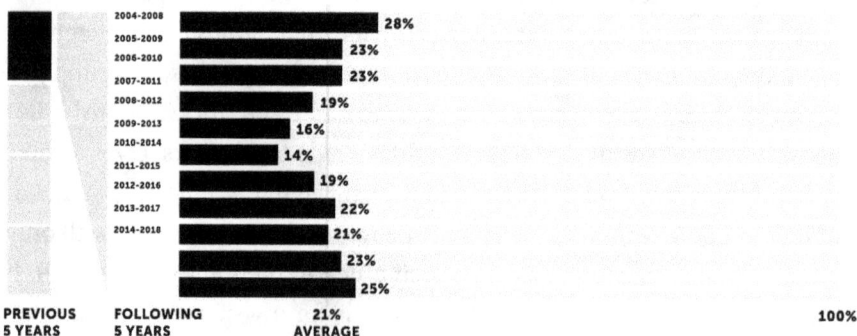

US-domiciled mutual fund data is from the CRSP Survivor-Bias-Free US Mutual Fund Database, provided by the Center for Research in Security Prices, University of Chicago

That's why these funds have to find another way to "beat" the market. Otherwise, it wouldn't take long for investors to leave—maybe after just two or three years of a disappointing fund. How they get around this problem is by offering numerous funds. Every single mutual fund firm does this, and it's not just because they're trying to accommodate clients with different budgets and goals. It's because one will do better than the others, a fact the firm can then use to their considerable advantage.

Say you talk to a fund manager tomorrow and tell them you're looking to invest. They'll tell you about a portfolio that includes a range of different options, and you might notice that there are multiple choices in the same category. For instance, Fund A and Fund B are both focused on large-cap stocks, though they list different management teams and have slightly different descriptions of how they find opportunity in their sector. Over time, the parent company is going to collapse one of those funds. Whichever is the more disappointing of the two, they will take that pile of investor money and roll it into the other. Here is where the trickery happens.

Say Fund B achieves 10% returns every year for three years, while Fund A has a negative 10% return every year for three years. Does the firm admit defeat with Fund A and send investors the remainder of their money back? No, they take that money, put it in Fund B, and let the investors know the good news. They simply send you a letter that says something to the effect of "Here at XXXX fund, we have chosen to take advantage of economies of scale and similar investment objectives, so we are merging these two funds to better serve our investors." But what they really do is kill one fund, and roll the money to the fund with the better historical performance.

In that case, what would you say should happen to the poor rates of return from the fund that was closed, to accurately track the results of investors over time? What might make sense from a mathematical perspective is to perform some kind of average of the performance rates of the two funds being combined. That is not what happens. The poor performance goes away. When you look at your next statement, despite the poor performance in reality, what you see from the mutual fund is a new three-year history that shows a positive 10% a year for the last three years. Of course, it comes off as good news. Even though the other option was a disappointment, Fund B is sure to do much better. After all, it gave the other investors 10% returns every year for three years—"beating" the market. The problem is that if Fund B doesn't do well, it will be cannibalized, too, and put into Fund C or Fund D. Then the Fund B investors would have received a similar story.

At no point does the firm need to adjust their rate of return on any of their funds to explain how they're really reaching it. In other words, they're taking full advantage of survivorship bias. It's like the report card from a college student who drops a class they are failing before it affects their GPA. If you have ever received a notice that one of your mutual fund holdings was being merged with another, know that identifying your true rates of return over time is no simple task.

Shiny Object Syndrome

Active managers make a great effort to help their investors *feel* good at all times, even if what is going on under the surface of their portfolios is far from favorable. Let us be the first to warn you that if you are going to employ the kind of portfolio strategy that is based in real research, you need to accept that you're going to be dissatisfied with some part of your portfolio, 100% of the time.

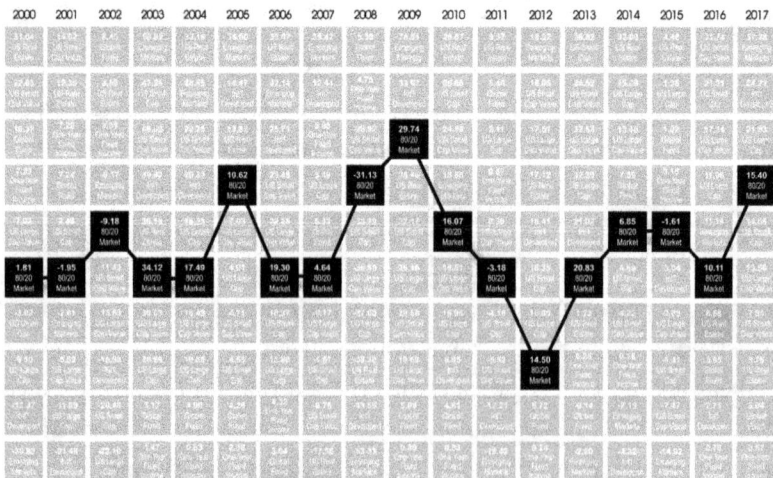

DIVERSIFIED 80/20 PORTFOLIO QUILT CHART
Annual Return (%), Blended Benchmarks

(This looks even better in color! Go to www.YBYWbook.com to check it out!

As you can see in the chart, each asset class can perform wildly different in any given year. So, there's always going to be someone or something that outperforms your academically allocated, globally diversified portfolio. This will happen every year, without fail, and there will always be that one asset class that is just skyrocketing.

You might think that investing in the current hot sector would be an easy temptation to avoid, but these opportunities, those which are "too good to be true," have been the ruin of many people's finances. Let's go back to what happened during the infamous tech bubble that burst in 2000, and look at the general public, not just the dentists who closed their practices to day-trade.

Leading up to that massive downturn, because of the amazing growth of stocks in the tech sector, investors became dissatisfied with seeing only single-digit annual returns. After all, when they looked over at their friends making 300% returns in the NetNet fund (not kidding, this was an actual fund), single digits seemed like they were for suckers. So they pulled out of their investments and invested in tech startups and NASDAQ indexes.

We know so many people who lost their shirt this way in the early 2000s. In that same decade, if you had created an academically allocated, globally diversified portfolio—the kind of investment strategy we recommend for all of our clients—you would have made it through the tech bubble with less than a 10% loss. That's not great, but imagine all the people who saw those shiny tech stocks and left their portfolios altogether. They would have traded a 9% loss for an 80% cratering of the NASDAQ that completely destroyed their entire portfolio by the end of 2000.

Real estate saw similar rates of appreciation during the mid-2000s. Academically allocated, globally diversified portfolios performed well prior to the 2008 financial crisis, but they were not getting 50% appreciation like the leveraged real estate opportunities that seemed to exist in every city across the country. Thus, investors flooded money into risky real estate. Since most people's previous experience in real estate was limited to buying their own home, they didn't really understand how much more risk they were taking. Because of the leverage of such deals, these investors didn't simply lose a percentage of their invested capital; they

GROWTH OF WEALTH

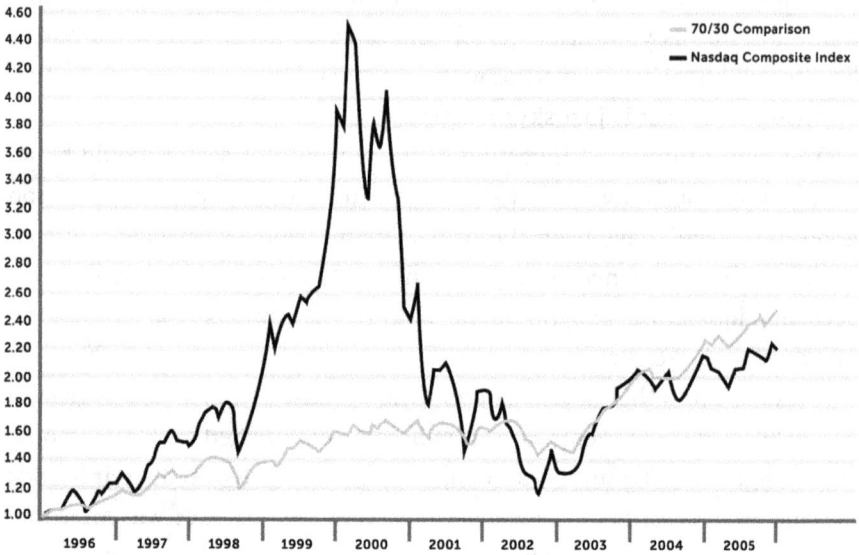

still owed the bank more than the value of all of their real estate even after eating the loss.

While we may be critical of this kind of "shiny object" thinking, we want to stress how common it is—even among people who otherwise make smart decisions. Many investors even ignored their well-intentioned financial advisors who implored them to ignore the temptation to radically overhaul their entire strategies for just one asset. We know of some advisors who lost clients over it, because these clients were only enjoying modest returns while their friends "got rich" in the real estate market.

Your financial planning requires a long-term perspective—one that precludes you from chasing the many shiny objects that will grab your attention between now and retirement. If you can't bear skipping the party, just protect yourself. We suggest limiting your investment in those "hot opportunities" to a minority percentage of your capital at work.

Your financial planning also requires building discipline, a muscle we'll need to exercise in order to hold strategy in both good times and bad.

That means avoiding concentrated positions in "hot stocks" like Facebook, Apple, Amazon, Netflix, and others that seem like they can do no wrong. As always, the pendulum will eventually swing in the other direction, and those who enjoy boasting about their shiny objects now will loathe being reminded of them later.

SPECIAL NOTE: As we go to print, we are in the midst of the COVID-19 stay-at-home orders. This environment reminds us that in addition to avoiding "shiny object syndrome," there is equal importance in holding strategy, especially during periods where all you might see are daily fearful headlines from the media.

Leveraging Your Human Capital in the Market

Many active managers attempt to beat the market by outsmarting it from the inside. Academic evidence abounds that investors (whether they are active fund managers or individuals) cannot predictably outperform the market over time. This doesn't mean that better-than-market returns cannot be achieved over time; it just means they cannot be achieved in the public financial market. But whether you are looking to outperform the market somewhere else—like in your business—or you are beginning to harvest some of your business gains and build diversity in the financial markets, there is one vital resource that is often ignored: your *human capital.* Our human capital is what we bring to the table to add value to the equation beyond just the money involved. This includes assets like education, training, and intelligence. For extra-market investing, there is a whole world of opportunities to employ your *human capital* to create attractive returns.

For market-based investing, we have identified only three skills that make up the core of your human capital as it relates to stock market investing. The list is short because there are no "super powers" in the world of public stock market investing. In public markets, all information is supposed to be equally available to all participants. Special advantages have labels like "insider trading" and are illegal. However, there are a few key abilities you can develop that are freely available to anyone, and widely neglected by most investors.

Dalbar (a top mutual fund research firm) has shown that most individual stock market investors underperform inflation over the long term. Dalbar points to investor behavior as the lead factor in this consistent underperformance. We agree, and our assertion is that the three skills discussed below are the solution to the problem of underperformance.

DALBAR: 20-YEAR ANNUALIZED RETURNS (1996-2015)

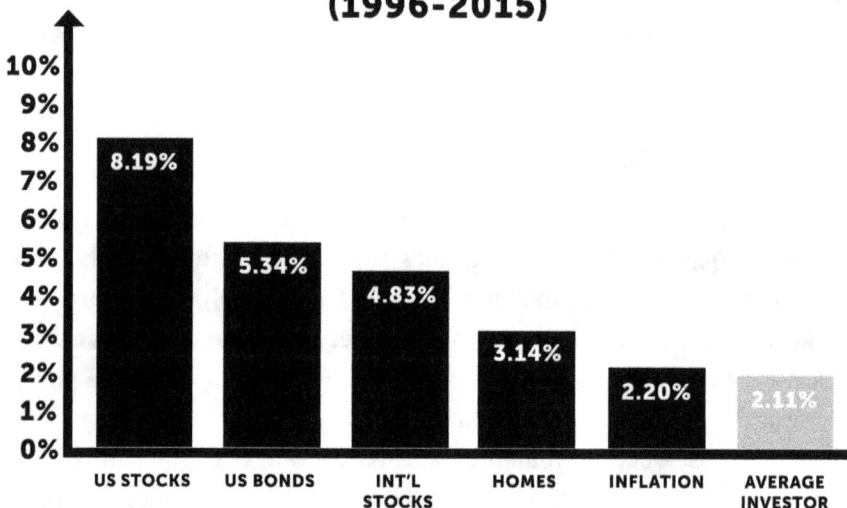

	Return
US STOCKS	8.19%
US BONDS	5.34%
INT'L STOCKS	4.83%
HOMES	3.14%
INFLATION	2.20%
AVERAGE INVESTOR	2.11%

US Stocks: S&P 500 Total Return Index; US Bonds: Barclays US Aggregate Bond Total Return Index; International Stocks: MSCI EAFE Total Return Index; Homes: U.S. existing home sales median price; Inflation: CPI-U; Average Investor: Average Asset Allocation Investor from "Quantitative Analysis of Investor Behavior, 2016" Dalbar, Inc. www.dalbar.com

1. **Tolerate Volatility:** When investors put capital at risk, returns are the reward for braving that uncertain future. Markets need money, and markets reward those who can hold back fear when short-term obstacles appear.
2. **Rebalance:** A portfolio must be consistently rebalanced over time to maintain its appropriate asset allocations. That means taking money from your asset classes that have grown the fastest, and transferring it to the underperformers, so you don't become dangerously over-represented in one area. Said another way, you are selling high in one category in order to buy low in another.

3. **Discipline:** Not enough people understand the importance of this skill. As an investor, you are rewarded for your patience and time in the market. Even without any volatility, you need patience to succeed with investing. Self-indulgence is thinking about how you feel, then doing what is going to feel good right now. Self-discipline forces us to think about the future we will have given the actions (not always pleasant at the time) we need to take, then feeling good about the results of our actions. Most people don't have discipline. The largest wealth transfers occur from those who are undisciplined and impatient to those who are disciplined and patient. Those of us who can be the latter will slowly accumulate larger slices of the pie over time.

Understanding Your Rate of Return

To finish this chapter, we want you to know that it is critically important to understand *where* your returns are coming from before you get too excited about any new opportunity to invest. It's possible, even likely, that there will be at least one opportunity in the future that raises plenty of red flags but still feels too alluring to resist. This is where shiny object syndrome starts to combine with the entrepreneur's trap. You might start to convince yourself that *this* isn't the same thing as a bubble. *This* isn't like that other "opportunity" that cleaned out your buddy. *This* is going to be different, and you'd be a fool to pass it up.

Let's assume that if you have an academically allocated, globally diversified portfolio, you can expect to earn an 8% average annual rate of return over the next 10 years. This is a reasonable assumption, though there are also plenty of 10-year spans where the returns have been above or below 8%. Nonetheless, let's assume that 8% return.

Why, then, would we decide to put any money in a bank certificate of deposit (CD) that only promises a 2% rate of return over the next five years? The reason is that those returns are definitely going to be smooth sailing up and to the right of the graph. There will be no ups and downs at all. You just have to deposit your money and wait. Risk is never going to be an issue. Because the return is so safe and predictable, the bank doesn't have to offer a very high rate of return. People looking for very secure parking spots for their money will gladly accept.

A CD isn't an object that is very shiny, alluring, or entertaining, though. What about those one-of-a-kind opportunities that just seem to land in your lap—not the entire market? The apartment building that's being constructed and could "easily" give you a 30% rate of return in just a few years. Or trust deed lending that requires no work at all but could be worth a 13% rate of return in the relatively near future. Or the software start-up that could literally change your life if you can just part with $100,000 for a year or so.

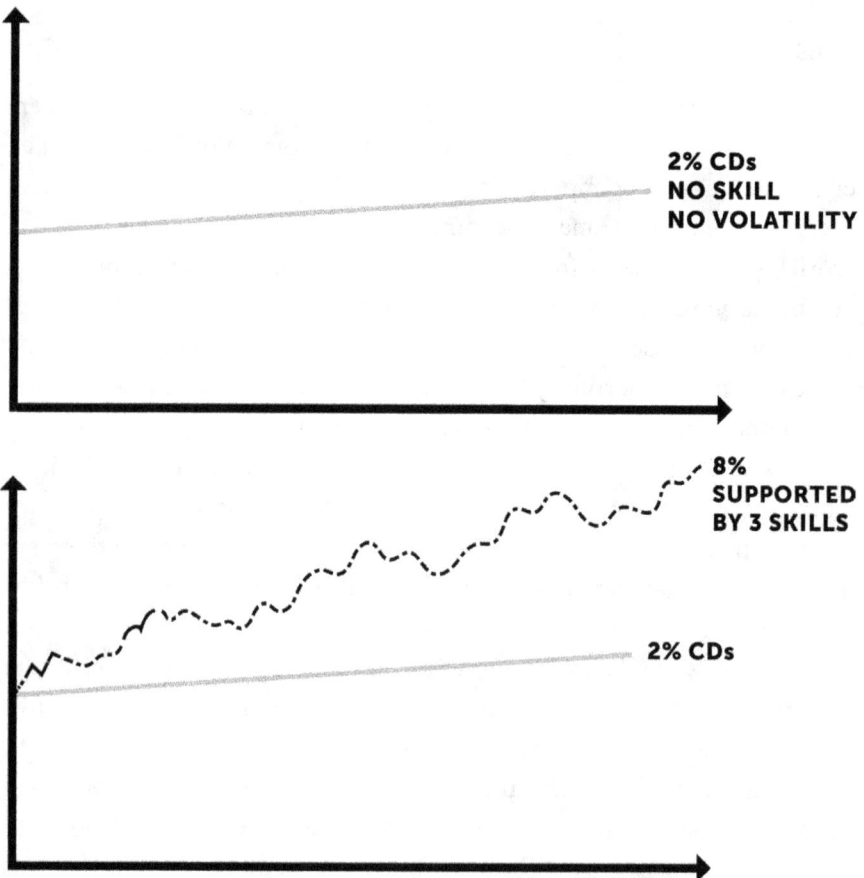

2% CDs
NO SKILL
NO VOLATILITY

8%
SUPPORTED
BY 3 SKILLS

2% CDs

Why opt for a measly 8% when these incredible opportunities are out there waiting for you? Because there are only two reasons they can ever offer such high returns.

The first is if you truly bring something to the table. That's your human capital. It's an asset that the other investors desperately need, which is why they are offering you such incredible returns. They want to entice you to take part in the deal because they know your human capital will go a long way toward ensuring its success—or just allowing it to happen in the first place.

For example, Paul has a friend who flips houses on the side, and he sees much higher returns than 8% from his efforts. However, that's because he understands every single step of the process. It's because he's willing to leave his wife and kids at home while he goes out and supervises all of the work that needs to be done until the house can be put back out on the market and start bringing in revenue.

If you have similar expertise or talent, then you have human capital you can deploy, which is the best way to seek to outperform market returns. You may have other traits that serve the same role. Maybe you're just able to invest a much larger sum of money than anyone else. As the other investors want your contribution, they're willing to offer you greater returns in exchange. Similarly, maybe you're an accredited investor, giving you access to pools most others can't enter. You might just have valuable connections that a group of investors knows they can leverage to improve their chances of success.

There are countless other ways you could bring something to the table, but rest assured, if none of them apply to you, there's only one other way you can possibly beat the market: taking more risk. This probably seems obvious. If you're willing to put money in an extremely speculative investment, you can also expect a much bigger payoff—if it actually turns out to be a winner.

For the most part, trying to outperform the market returns in individual stocks is akin to speculation and gambling. Assuming you don't have some high level of knowledge that works as a competitive edge, you're just hoping the odds work out in your favor. To be fair, they certainly can.

It's just impossible to plan for that level of speculation. Understandably, most people also don't want to gamble with their financial futures. If anything, they're looking for the surest of sure things.

Unfortunately, people don't always realize when they're gambling. This is especially true among us entrepreneurs. We're accustomed to constantly bringing value to the table. Our success also largely depends on being self-taught. There's no boss above us to ensure we receive sufficient training or understand the industry well enough.

Nonetheless, it is important to understand what exactly you bring to the table. If someone else is offering you a deal, it is even more vital that you understand *what they see you bringing to the table*. If you can't identify it, then you're not actually being brought to the table. You're being served to it—on a silver platter.

For example, you might be invited into a real estate deal even though you don't have any experience with that industry other than owning a home. It turns out, the reason you've been "invited" is because your rate of return is small relative to the amount you're being asked to put in. You might need $100,000 to get involved, whereas the person organizing the deal is only contributing $20,000. While they certainly want the deal to succeed, they have a lot less to lose if it doesn't.

At the same time, if it does succeed, they might be pocketing just as much as you would. Their risk-to-reward ratio is much better than yours. Now, if you bring this up, you'll generally get the response that they're contributing "sweat equity." Be that as it may, just remember that sweat is cheap. Equity is not. Therefore, while they might have an impressive amount of human capital, it also doesn't require nearly as much financial risk. Your lack of human capital in this situation means your contribution is solely money-based.

Seem fair? It might. We've known people who enter into these kinds of situations knowingly. They assume it's fair, because if not for the other person's knowledge, there would be no deal at all.

That might be true, but think about this: Why don't these other investors just go to a bank for the money they need? It would be much more affordable to pay a bank something around 7% interest instead of offering you a 10%, 20%, or even 30% return. It's because no bank would take the deal! Any informed advisor would take one look at it and know that it's much too speculative. The same goes for any other educated investor. At the very least, they would require some kind of collateral to better protect their position.

Therefore, if you're being highly compensated for your monetary contribution—not one of human capital—and you can't find the risk you're taking to deserve it, then you're in trouble, because the risk is there. You just haven't found it yet.

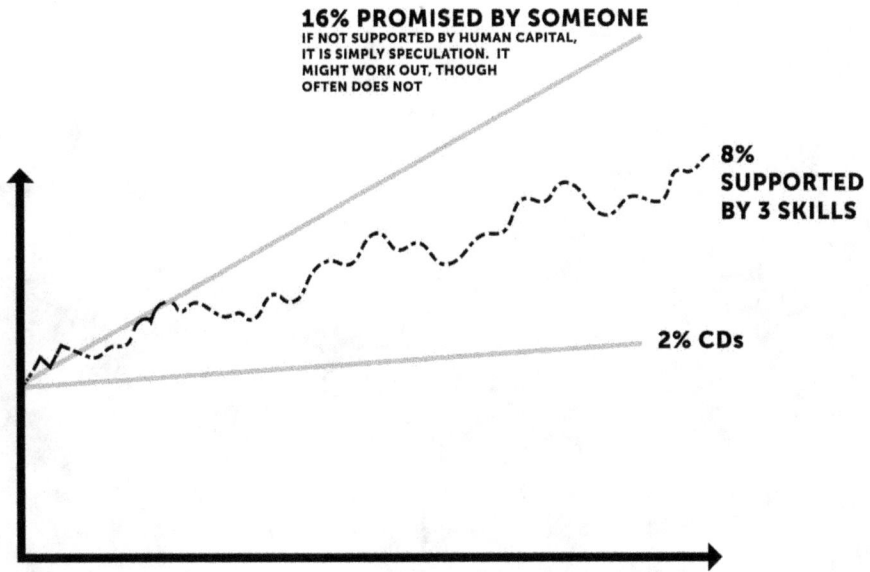

16% PROMISED BY SOMEONE
IF NOT SUPPORTED BY HUMAN CAPITAL,
IT IS SIMPLY SPECULATION. IT
MIGHT WORK OUT, THOUGH
OFTEN DOES NOT

8% SUPPORTED BY 3 SKILLS

2% CDs

Let's return to real estate one more time: How many investors have you heard say things like, "God's not making any more of it" or "There will always be renters." Those statements are both objectively true, and we are not suggesting all real estate deals are bad. Our firm helps clients assess and enter into real estate purchases all the time.

However, many investors have come into those kinds of deals with no understanding of the market, just a massive sum of money because they have listened to this "expert" advice, which seems demonstrably true and looks like quite the guarantee. How could anything go wrong? Well, as many investors have had to learn the hard way, that kind of advice can cost you your investment and put you into massive debt.

In the last part of the book, we're going to return to the investment you have the most control over, the one where your human capital can beat out the market. We're talking, of course, about your business and what you need to do to make sure it will come out with a great return.

PART 3:
MAKE THE MOST OUT OF THE BUSINESS YOU'VE BUILT

Chapter 7:
Think Your Business Has Value?
Then Prove It Every Year

THROUGHOUT THIS BOOK, WE'VE REVISITED THE FACT THAT HOW MUCH you value your business isn't important. It might be a point of pride, which is fine, but in terms of how the market will value it, your opinion doesn't count.

This is where a lot of business owners get themselves in trouble. To them, their business is worth a fortune, maybe even several fortunes. It can be an extremely abrupt rush of reality when they find out that other people don't think the same thing.

Finding Out What Your Company Is Actually Worth

In all the years of our combined experience, we've seen only a small handful of instances where a client already had an independent valuation of their company before meeting us. Most will tell us how much they believe it's worth and, to be fair, they'll usually offer some good reasons for that assumption other than that's just what they want for their business. Nonetheless, an assumption isn't necessarily reality. Even the few times clients have had valuations done, they were at least two years old. While their answer isn't an assumption, it's still more of an educated guess than the objective truth. When it comes to your financial independence, you definitely don't want there to be any ambiguity on the numbers.

Getting an independent valuation is one of the best decisions you can make, for yourself and for your business. We know you're busy and that you already have plenty of demands competing for your cash flow. Aside from trusting their own intuition about its value, time and money are the two other reasons most business owners cite for not having a valuation done. They already have enough going on and they don't want a new item on their annual budget, especially one that will cost $2,000 to $9,000 dollars a year.

However, let's look at this from another perspective. As you know, most people don't have companies to sell in order to pay for their retirement. Instead, they're depending on mutual funds or some kind of retirement plan. Like you, they're not checking every month or even every year to see if these investments are headed in the right direction. That might not be wise, but these people also aren't concentrating their net worth in one single company like you are. They're invested in a number of different companies. It's this approach that offers stability and probably makes them feel comfortable not checking in on the value of their portfolio on a regular basis. And of course all they need to do to find out that value is type in one login and password at one website, and their account values are there, updated on a daily basis.

In your case, we're talking about a single privately held company. Imagine it wasn't yours for a moment. Imagine you had millions of dollars in someone else's company—say, a local retail shop. How often would you check in to see how much your share of the business was worth? If it were a publicly traded company, you'd probably check the share price almost every single day—maybe multiple times a day. You have a lot riding on its value. However, even if it were a private company, wouldn't you check in at least once a year? With all your money tied up in this one single business, would you consider doing it even more often?

Why do so many business owners not know such a crucial fact about their companies? As we covered, part of it has to do with the fact that many are simply overconfident in how much their business is worth. They assume they already know. However, there are two other very important reasons.

The first is actually the exact opposite of the one we just covered. Many business owners think they know how much their company is worth, but they're worried it won't be enough. They'd rather put off having the value assessed until they:

- Finish the new initiative.
- Get through the next quarter of sales.
- Bring in that new manager who is going to turn that department around.
- Roll out the new marketing that will increase sales and decrease cost.

It's the Schrödinger's cat of valuations. Until the owner actually checks, the result could go either way (and in the owner's mind, the way is always positive). Unfortunately, if the value isn't going to be enough for retirement, that's not a problem that goes away on its own. Ignoring it virtually guarantees the pain will get much worse. If this is the reason holding you back, please make it a priority. The sooner you do, the sooner you can turn things around if need be.

The second reason we alluded to earlier is the cost involved. Sound Financial Group has a client whose company employs only about 10 people, yet it produces a little more than $1 million a year in revenue. When we first started working with this client, we immediately recommended that he pay a CPA to assess the value of his company, and continue to do so every year or two.

It is easy to quickly abandon a strategy like this when looking at the cost. Let's say that cost in this example is $5,000 for the appraisal. That can seem like a recurring expense to be avoided, not embraced. But compared to the value of the company, the cost of the appraisal is only a tiny fraction: 0.5%. And there is more to be learned from an appraisal than just the value of the company. You also get to learn how to increase the value of your company.

If you want to have an analytics-based valuation of your business done, go to www.YBYWbook.com and fill out the online form to receive a business valuation (we will be providing a limited amount of these free to our readers).

Do You Know How to Make Your Company Worth More?

The biggest misconception about having your company's value assessed is that it's an expense with no real return on investment (ROI). Many owners think that unless the assessment raises a massive red flag, they'll be tossing money in the trash—at least until it's actually time to sell.

Nothing could be further from the truth. Business owners who regularly check to see how much their companies are worth benefit from finding out how to make them worth even more—to themselves and to a future buyer.

Built to Sell by John Warrillow is a great book about a business owner who works to create a company that can thrive without him, because he knows that will make it extremely attractive to a prospective buyer. However, once he was successful at building such a business, he didn't want to sell it. Sure, he'd have no problem finding a buyer, but the company was now worth far more to him.

The main thing to remember about the ROI in regular valuations is this: if you don't know what your business is worth and why, you won't know how to make it worth more—for yourself or a future buyer.

Know Your Role and Create Your Hive

What role do you play in your business? You're the owner, right? What other hats are you still wearing at the moment? Just as important, what role *should* you play? If your goal is to eventually sell your business for as much money as possible, you must answer these questions.

One of our favorite business finance authors out there is Mike Michalowicz. We've already mentioned his book *Profit First*, which is a fantastic resource for any business owner. Mike was even kind enough to join us on some episodes of the *Your Business Your Wealth* podcast. Another book we highly recommend from Mike is *Clockwork*, which has a great subtitle that really gets at the heart of our topic in this section: *Design Your Business to Run Itself.*

If you don't get your company to a place where it's running like clockwork *without* you, what are you really trying to sell a buyer? You'd be trying to sell them a job. Would *you* ever want to buy a job?

The first step to making your company run like clockwork is getting clear about all the roles you play. You might just be a business owner, but you might also be CEO, or president and CEO. Maybe you also handle the books, or you're the chief salesperson. Take an inventory of all the hats you wear, then assign yourself a salary for each role.

Think of it from a potential buyer's point of view. If they buy your company, they'll take your business owner hat, but what if you were the head of sales, too? Well, they'll need to hire someone to do that, which means paying them a wage. If you weren't paying yourself, their salary as the business owner just took a massive hit. These are the kinds of considerations a potential buyer will make when assessing your company. The more hats you wear without taking money out of revenues to pay yourself, the less your business is actually going to be worth to a buyer.

Again, a shrewd buyer doesn't want to pay for a job, much less several of them. Don't sell yourself short on your salary, either. If you're acting as the manager of a retail store you own, don't pay yourself $35,000 a year when you know the going rate is $50,000. If you don't need the money right now, it can go into your Wealth Coordination Account to buy other assets and support your financial future.

Regardless, if you try selling your business with that subpar salary, buyers will realize they'll probably need to find another $150,000 a year in order to replace you as manager. Taking this same idea one level higher: if you are paying yourself profit and salary of $350,000 as the owner/CEO of your company, but you are really also serving as the president and operations manager for no compensation, the prospective buyer is going to know that they will have to find another $100,000 to $150,000 a year of cash flow to replace you.

Another reason why we love *Clockwork* is its take on how to set up your business so it's systematized around the human capital you bring to the table. If you've ever read *The E-Myth Revisited* by Michael Gerber, you know that this is the opposite of what he recommends. Gerber is adamant that you actually systematize the lowest roles in your company first. While we are big fans of Gerber and love his book, we actually prefer the approach described in *Clockwork.*

That idea is based on the queen bee of a hive. In a hive, the entire colony operates in support of the queen. That doesn't mean she has to completely run the hive, though. Instead, she has one very specific role—to lay eggs. If she doesn't perform this job, the rest of the hive will replace her with another bee who will. However, as long as the queen does her job, the rest of the colony will perform all the other tasks required to keep her fed and safe, as well as ensure the entire hive is operational. Link to resource page: _YBYWbook.com_.

In terms of your business, we encourage you to discover and define your queen-bee role. Then, you need to make sure the rest of your workforce is structured around supporting that human capital. You must be able to take everything else off of your plate, so you can focus on this one talent or expertise.

Once you do this, the next step is figuring out how to democratize that role throughout your company so that the key activities of that role are happening throughout company. Replace yourself as an "employee" who does one job, so you can transition to working _on_ your business and not _in_ it, as we talked about in chapter 1.

Business Continuity Plan: Protection from the Worst-Case Scenario

Another vital way of protecting your company's value is to create a business continuity plan. This plan's goal is exactly what it sounds like. You want to make sure that, after a disruptive event that makes normal operations impossible, your company can continue to function and make money.

Think about the businesses in New York City whose employees couldn't even get into their buildings for a year or more after Hurricane Sandy. While it must have been extremely inconvenient for all of them, at least those with business continuity plans had contingencies they could leverage to get back up and running. Those that didn't were forced to contend with the challenges of handling the aftermath of a hurricane and figuring out where they could reopen to reinitiate their cash flow ASAP.

A thorough business continuity plan doesn't just cover what your company should do if a natural disaster destroys your main site of operation, either. One of its most important jobs is outlining what should happen if you can't be present for a prolonged period of time.

As an example, you could find yourself stuck overseas for any number of reasons. In that case, who is in charge during your absence? Who can handle payroll and write the checks? How can you ensure operations don't cease?

There are other scenarios to think about, as well. You could become disabled to the point where you literally are no longer able to perform your duties. A loved one could become sick and need your attention for weeks or even months. If these things were to happen, your replacement—whether temporary or permanent—would be very grateful to open a document that outlines their new role and describes how to perform its various tasks.

Is a Buy/Sell Agreement Best?

For those of you who are operating with a partner, just as important as a business continuity plan is some kind of agreement about what will happen to the ownership of your company if one of you passes away or otherwise leaves.

Most partnerships have a buy/sell agreement to address this. It outlines under what conditions each partner would need for someone to buy their shares and under what conditions each partner would be willing to buy them. It may also stipulate who exactly is approved to buy a departing partner's shares and what events can lead to a buyout (for example, retirement or death). In a lot of ways, it's like a prenuptial agreement for business partners.

If you already have a buy/sell agreement, or if you are thinking of getting yours done, you may want to consider if selling is at all what you want. You may want a "keep in the family" agreement. One reason many partners opt for these agreements is that they know of examples where a buy/sell agreement forced partners to sell the company and, while that was happening, one of them died. Without a "keep in the family agreement" in place, that partner's children had no right to succeed them in the company.

Before you rush right to a buy/sell agreement with your partner, sit down and have a frank conversation. Maybe, the right move is to decide that, in the event that a partner dies, the one who survives will go from earning 50% ownership to 75%, with the remaining 25% going to the deceased partner's family, leaving the spouse the ability to profit from the company's continued success and allowing the deceased partner's children to participate in their parent's legacy. Whatever the case, this needs to be detailed in an official buy/sell agreement.

This is also why defined roles with their own salaries are so important. If the deceased was acting as a business owner and CEO, the family needs to understand that they're only receiving compensation relative to the business owner's dividend (K-1) distributions. That's because a new CEO will need to be hired and paid.

We know of actual situations where no formal agreement was in place, so the surviving partner had to continue running their business with a new partner—the person who was married to the deceased. In fact, there have even been times when the surviving partner had to share their company with the deceased partner's ex-spouse because the divorce wasn't finalized. The deceased's children (or stepchildren) could become partners, as well, because of how their estate planning documents were worded.

Far more common, though, are handshake agreements among partners where they pledge to take care of the other one's family if anything should happen to them. Unfortunately, because there's no formal agreement about paying out the spouse at a certain rate, they're only entitled to the owner distribution—which will be far less. In this example, someone loses their partner and has to adjust to going from living off $500,000 a year to just $200,000 a year. It doesn't take long before the spouse needs a loan from the surviving partner. Even in situations where those two treat each other like family, that's going to make for a very awkward relationship going forward.

Another costly mistake to avoid with a buy/sell agreement is allowing the sale of your business to be formula-driven. It has to be sold for 10 times profit, 2 times revenue, or some other arbitrary calculation. The reason this doesn't work in the wake of a tragedy is that the two families who were otherwise on the same side of the table leading up to this event are now pulling in opposite directions.

One wants to get the most. One wants to pay the least. One has the uncertainty of still carrying a million-dollar payroll every year. One just wants money on their balance sheet because they have a family to feed without the certainty of a regular paycheck coming in.

A much better alternative is the annual appraisal we covered earlier—ideally by a third party. The value should then be recorded in the minutes and shared with the spouses of each partner. By doing this every year, while both partners are still alive, everyone is on the same side of the table. Both have the same interest in the transaction. This will make dealing with distributions much easier in the event of a partner's death, because it will be based on a value everyone agreed to when both were still alive and pulling in the same direction.

Whether you are planning on writing a buy/sell agreement that fully purchases your partner's share in the business or that partially buys them out, allowing the family to remain involved in the business with minority interest, you can fund this agreement ahead of time with insurance. Many partners use life and disability insurance to create the capital needed to execute this buyout, without having to worry about what happens to the business cash flows while they are trying to buy out the partners.

If you do go down the path of funding the buy/sell agreement with insurance, you may also want to consider if you and your partner are also key employees. If so, you may want to own a multiple of your salary in insurance, so that the company itself has additional liquidity beyond the buy/sell to hire an employee who can carry the water that the partner was carrying previously. There are several tax considerations when executing something like this, so it is important that you focus in with your team to create the proper legal structures and select the most efficient life insurance.

Don't Let Your Friendship Keep You from the Smart Decision

We know that some of you are so close with your business partners that as you are reading right now, you are thinking that none of this applies to you. You know that if you pass away or go on disability and can't work anymore, your partner will do the right thing. Just like you would do the same for them and their family.

We understand where you're coming from and applaud the mutual trust you and your partner have for each other. However, having worked closely with other business clients for a very long time, we've seen many wonderful partnerships face unforeseen events that would leave you without a reliable way to fund your family's life.

For example, imagine if your business partner decides last minute to take their eldest daughter skiing somewhere for a week, instead of sticking around and helping you with a big project required to bring on a large new customer. Even after you explain the importance of digging into the project together, they decide to go while you stay back and double your hours to get the proposal ready in time.

During the trip, your business partner gets injured badly enough that they're no longer able to come into work every day and do their job. Are you going to be as apt to pay your non-contributing partner hundreds of thousands of dollars a year, especially when they caused the problem by doing something you explicitly asked them not to? If not, you might even have to fire your friend from whatever role they play (VP of sales, for example), so you can hire someone else. At the very least, this is going to cut their yearly paycheck until you can figure out how to buy them out.

We recommend avoiding handshake agreements, even among the closest of friends, because avoiding that kind of informal arrangement can also be the ultimate sign of respect. You're showing your business partner that you know memories can fade and interpretations can differ over time, so you want them, their family, and your relationship to be protected no matter what.

In *The Speed of Trust*, Stephen M. R. Covey has a great take on this subject. He strongly recommends writing things down, not because you don't trust the commitment of the other person, but rather to announce *your* commitment to the other person beyond your current feelings and the vagaries of your memory, which can eventually fail everyone. As a Chinese proverb says, the faintest ink is stronger than the best memory.

Chapter 8:
Retirement Plans for You
and Your Employees

THERE IS NO SUCH THING AS EMPLOYEE BENEFITS. EVERYTHING ABOUT adding an employee to your business, including their wages, should be a net benefit to you as the employer. Compensating your employees properly motivates them to bring value to your business. Most business owners do enjoy the satisfaction of creating jobs and making a positive impact in their employees' lives, yet if you as the employer are not benefiting from what you offer your employees, then such benefits will not be sustainable. Over time, it could put you in the position to terminate employees, grow far slower, run less profitably—or worse.

Thus, all of the benefits your company offers need to be *employer* benefits. This is not a matter of semantics, either. If you make the mistake of believing the common misconception about employee benefits, that decision has probably cost you more than it needed to, and will continue to do so in the future.

A Brief History of Employee Benefits

In the United States, the rise of employee benefits was actually an outcome of World War II. During this tumultuous time, the government passed laws it hoped would help stabilize the economy. Among other things, this meant that companies were not allowed to increase their employees' salaries. In effect, everyone's wages were frozen. The hope was that this would address the labor shortage caused by diverting so many people into military service. Otherwise, the government feared that employers would just continue raising salaries to compete for better workers, and inflation would start burning through the dollar's value. Almost any circumstance was worth avoiding another Great Depression for those who still remembered it.

One of the unforeseen consequences of Executive Order 9250, which established the Office of Economic Stabilization, was that freezing wages didn't keep companies from competing. Employers just got smarter at attracting the best talent by offering to pay for their health insurance instead. Although such coverage had already existed for more than a decade, this was the beginning of what we now refer to as "employee benefits." Of course, seen in this light, these insurance packages were more like employer benefits. While they provided insurance to employees, it was the employers who were really getting the most out of these offerings, by allowing them to secure top talent in a competitive market, and keep that talent healthy, productive, and able to show up to work.

Rethinking How You Compensate Your Workforce

Of course, we all want to keep the best possible people in our companies. But what if you no longer thought of benefits as the thing you need to put in place in order to keep the best possible people with your company?

In our experience, we have seen too many talent retention strategies that cost a lot and don't even measurably accomplish their intended goal. Therefore, we recommend that you think instead about what approach will help you the most as the owner. How can you compensate your employees in a way that results in the highest possible value to you and your employees in a cost-effective way? How can you keep employees productive and retain them, so that they're able to give your company the best possible shot at long-term financial success? This is where conventional wisdom regarding employee benefits falls short. Most employers just consider benefits as something they have to provide and don't actually think about how they can be used to improve their businesses.

Famous painter Pablo Picasso (1881–1973) once said, "Computers are useless. They only give you answers." While his age, relative to the advent of computers, surely contributed to his Luddite views, what he meant in this particular case was that asking the right questions is important, and that correct answers to the wrong questions can lead us in the wrong direction. You might ask, "What is the best 401(k) plan I can offer?" or "What do I need to do to offer better health insurance than my competitors?" But a more valuable question might be "What benefits could I offer to help develop better employees, deeper employee engagement, and a stronger company?" Sometimes this might just mean providing the marketplace standard. Other times, it may mean something more.

Offering a 401(k) Is Not Enough

Employee benefits have come a long way since World War II. In a changing job market, different industries have grown more and more creative in the range and types of benefits they offer, many designed to make the office feel like it has more amenities and comforts than the home. But the 401(k) has become one of the most common features of an employee benefits package. For most workers, health coverage and some kind of 401(k) with an employer match are a baseline expectation.

Nonetheless, as much as someone may appreciate having a match-based 401(k), no one has ever stuck with a company because of it. No one has ever rethought their decision to leave because they know their match will vest by another 20% after their next work anniversary. Neither are 401(k)s something most employees weigh heavily when considering positions with another company. Again, everyone appreciates having one, but it's also become the norm. It's just an expectation now. People aren't deciding to stay because the current employer's 401(k) is the most attractive 401(k) they can find.

At the end of the day, what most people look at is the same thing they did before World War II—how much will I make? Unfortunately, simply paying people more isn't always enough, either.

Raises Don't Retain

Salaries are clearly important, but the mistake most business owners make is thinking that's all employees care about. So, every year, they offer their best employees a higher paycheck and assume this will be sufficient to keep them on board.

In our experience, employees will not make the choice to leave or stay based on pure dollar compensation, unless the salary difference is exceedingly large, usually 20% or more. But even in the face of a large salary increase from a competitor, employees have a high likelihood of staying if elements like company culture, freedom, and autonomy are perceived to be greater with you. Your most valuable employees are likely smart enough to know that a 50% raise that they receive for only six months, before realizing their new company is an awful place to work, is no real raise.

Relying on raises can actually do more harm than good, too. That's because by paying your employees more, you're also increasing their perceived value to the market. Think about an actor. Once they make a couple of blockbuster hits and work up to negotiating a $20 million payday for a film, that becomes their new standard. Going forward, if a studio wants to hire them for a film, they know it's probably going to cost them that at least $20 million. Why? Because the actor has proven evidence that even $20 million is a worthwhile investment due to the returns they'll earn for the studio.

Translate that concept into one of your employees who is doing amazing work for you. As you want to keep them at your company, you decide to increase their paycheck from $100,000 to $120,000. That's a very sizable raise of 20%. Certainly, that should keep them from thinking about leaving, right? Perhaps.

However, you've also given them a great incentive to start looking elsewhere. After all, now they can sit down with a potential employer and tell them about the large sum of money they're making. That employer will also deduce that if you're paying them $120,000 a year, they must be doing work that is worth considerably more than that.

Have you ever been around someone who sprays on way too much cologne? Raises are like cologne: used in subtle and strategic doses, they can be a pleasant surprise. Lay it on too strong and you might find yourself suddenly all alone in the room.

The Power of a Deferred Compensation Agreement

The best way to keep an employee happy isn't to pay them more right now; it's to promise to pay them more in the future.

There is a limit to how effective that future promise can be, though. Most employees don't think 10 to 20 years down the line. The vast majority of people are much more adept at thinking about only the next three to five years. Through the power of deferred compensation agreements, we are going to help you map out a solution that maximizes the employees' perception of their compensation over the next three to five years without costing you anything more today.

Before we get into the details of a deferred compensation agreement, there is another approach to cover, because it tends to be even more popular. Keep in mind, popular is not always better.

When a business owner realizes one of their employees is a massive asset to their company, they often propose giving them a stake in the company. The idea is that by making them more than just an employee, that person will never think of leaving the company. If anything, they'll have every reason to stick around and improve its performance even more than before.

The first problem with this concept is that anytime you offer to make someone a partner, you are diluting your own value. However valuable that person is to the company now, they still won't eclipse the value you brought to the company in the earliest, riskiest years as shareholder number one. We are not saying it's absolutely never worth it—if the new partner increases the value of your company substantially, then it may have been the right move—but please don't make it the only move in your retention repertoire, and definitely don't make it the first.

The second issue is one that most business owners don't even think about until it's too late and, at that point, it represents a major misstep. They make their star employee a partner and then assume that person will now stay with the company until retirement. If they're wrong, they'll need to actually pay the departing partner for their share of the company. By trying to keep their star employee while saving some near-term cash, they end up creating a scenario where the employee gets far greater compensation for leaving, and the company takes a hit on cash flow.

That's why deferred compensation agreements are so lovely. They offer the best of both worlds—plenty of incentives for the employee to stick around and continue creating as much value as possible, while eliminating any concerns about destabilizing your own company. Remember: with a partner you are agreeing to pay them cash when they leave. With a deferred compensation agreement, you are paying them to stay.

A deferred compensation agreement is exactly what it sounds like. You agree to pay your employee a certain amount of money at a specific time, provided you don't terminate them. For example, let's take a look at that star employee who's making $100,000 per year. Instead of giving them a straight raise, you explain that you'll give them another $100,000 lump sum in five years if they continue to keep up their performance.

You can also use a formulaic increase to that future lump sum, tied to the company or the employee's specific performance. This is usually how it's done with salespeople, especially those relying largely on commission. No matter how you execute this, the goal is the same. Instead of spending more money now and increasing the employee's perceived value, you're deferring a large compensation for them once your company has received even greater returns from their work.

Keep in mind, there's no legal requirement that you set aside a certain amount every year, either. Therefore, if you promise someone $100,000 after five years, you don't actually have to keep setting aside $20,000 every year leading up to that deadline. You can just carry it on your balance sheet as a contingent deferred liability, which will be a great tax deduction when you pay it out to your employee.

Nonetheless, as that date for the increased compensation gets closer and closer, your employee will have all the more reason to continue adding more value to your company. They don't want anything to happen until that deferred compensation payout occurs.

You are probably thinking that once you pay that deferred bonus, they might think about leaving the very next day. That could be true; just like we talked about earlier, they can now go to another employer and explain that they're worth at least that much more to you, justifying an even higher offer from a competitor. This is why you start building the next 5-year deferred compensation agreement with them 6 to 12 months before the current one pays out. On the day that $100,000 payment arrives, they will already be smelling the one that is starting to cook over the next 5 years.

As wonderful a place as your company is to work, even your best, most hard-working employees may find reasons to grow dissatisfied over the span of five years or so. This is another huge advantage that deferred compensation agreements provide.

We recently worked with a publicly traded tech company that is going through a similar challenge. They offered one of their best employees this type of agreement four years ago. Since then, it had become clear that this star worker was becoming dissatisfied with his job and had considered leaving. Fortunately, that agreement kept him coming to work day after day and doing his best to keep his performance levels up. He didn't want to miss out on the large sum of money he had been guaranteed.

If not for that carrot out in front of him, he may have decided to transfer to another company a long time ago, which means his current employer would have lost years of outstanding work. Even better, by keeping him on, they still have time to address the issues that were causing him to think about going to a competitor, and he in turn has motivation to voice those issues. The company thus has the chance to try to find some solutions, which might mean finding him a new position or even giving him more responsibilities so he feels sufficiently challenged. Whatever the case, the company has a great opportunity to bring him back to the table and even offer him another plan to ensure he sticks around for five more years to come.

(As a quick side note, a deferred compensation agreement can be the ideal way to help ensure that a key employee will be the successor of your business. When the time comes to pay them their deferred compensation, you can give them the option of using it as a down payment toward the total they will pay you to buy your company.)

Now, consider the opposite example: an executive at a different publicly traded and very well-known company who doesn't have a deferred compensation agreement waiting for him. He's a top performer and shoulders a large amount of the culture and systems that make this company great. Everyone there loves him. But recently they hired a new CEO. For whatever reason, he just hasn't been a good fit, and the executive is having a really difficult time working with him.

What's keeping him there? Very little. He even has an impressive personal balance sheet, so he's not someone who needs that next paycheck. If he does decide to leave, not only will the company need to replace him, but they'll probably have a lot of work to do to rebuild the areas that were relying so heavily on his hard work.

The prudent move for that company would be to offer the executive a deferred compensation plan for at least a year. That might be more than enough time to figure out how to solve the problems that are making him think about leaving. Since there is not a plan in place right now, with his dim outlook on the future with that company, there is a lower and lower probability every day that he even musters the energy and takes the personal risk to voice these issues to the business owner. Most likely he just starts looking for other opportunities, which means when he leaves, the narrative is much easier for him, something like "I've really valued my time here, and I wasn't looking to leave, but this opportunity dropped into my lap that was too good to pass up, I'm sure you understand."

It's not so different from marriages. Many marriage counselors believe that the moment one spouse or the other begins thinking about leaving, the relationship is effectively over. It's very hard to turn things around at that point. By keeping the executive in place for even just a year, they're keeping him from getting "wandering eyes," and they're buying time to consider how they can resolve the issues.

The Psychological Benefits of a Deferred Compensation Agreement

Beyond practical considerations, there are still a number of other important psychological benefits associated with deferred compensation agreements. Specifically, the way deferred compensation plans are inter-preted by your employees will give you some very advantageous results. First and foremost, it changes how they feel they're being compensated in a positive way, despite the fact that you're not actually changing the amount aside from the deferred lump sum.

In other words, if you promise someone $100,000 after five years, they're going to feel like they're making an extra $20,000 every year, even though they're technically not. Said another way, to recruit them away, a competing employer would likely have to offer in excess of the $20,000 a year for the employee to feel like it was worth it to leave.

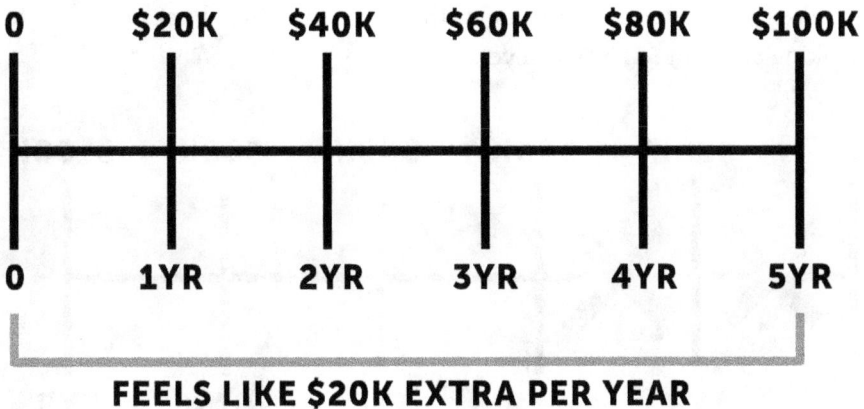

0	$20K	$40K	$60K	$80K	$100K

0	1YR	2YR	3YR	4YR	5YR

FEELS LIKE $20K EXTRA PER YEAR

After their first year, that's going to seem like an extra $25,000 a year. You see, that first year that has passed is now sunk cost to the executive, so to get a better offer, the next employer would have to pay them an addi-tional $25,000 per year.

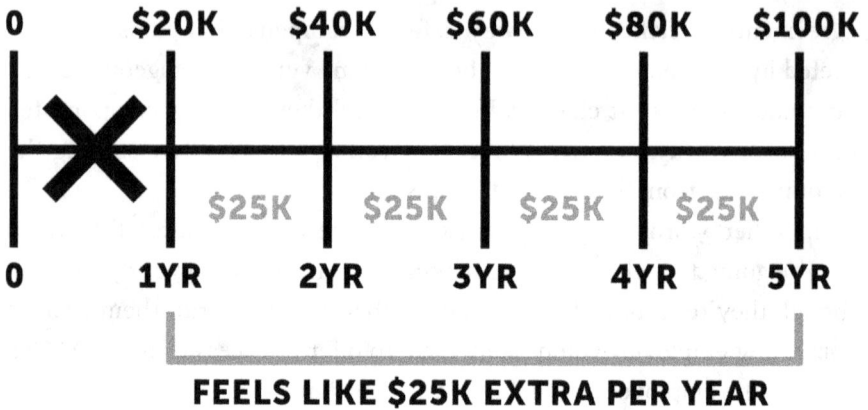

| 0 | $20K | $40K | $60K | $80K | $100K |

X

| $25K | $25K | $25K | $25K |

| 0 | 1YR | 2YR | 3YR | 4YR | 5YR |

FEELS LIKE $25K EXTRA PER YEAR

Two years after the agreement, they'll be thinking about how they're making an extra $33,333.33 a year.

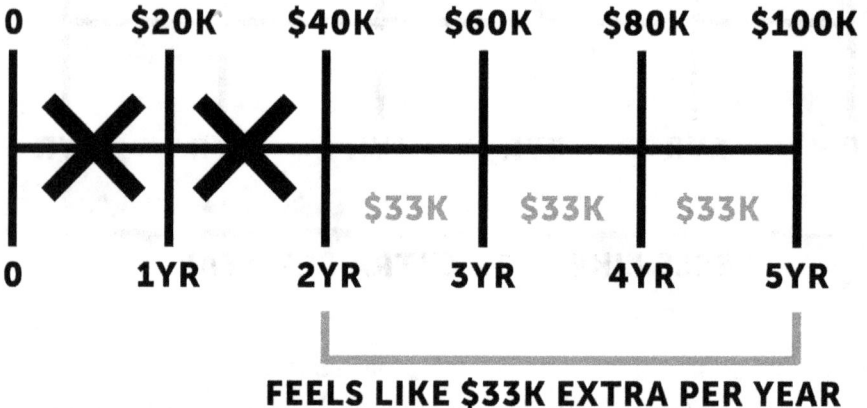

| 0 | $20K | $40K | $60K | $80K | $100K |

X X

| $33K | $33K | $33K |

| 0 | 1YR | 2YR | 3YR | 4YR | 5YR |

FEELS LIKE $33K EXTRA PER YEAR

The reason this is so important is that if someone wants to recruit them away from your company, they'll have to offer an amount that reflects this "extra" annual compensation. Otherwise, your employee wouldn't think about taking it. If they do, they leave $100,000 on the table. Imagine the conversation about compensation in the job interview with your competitor:

Company recruiting your employee: "What is the salary they are paying you?"

Employee: "They are paying me $100,000 a year, though they have this deferred compensation agreement in place that effectively pays me $33,000 more a year for the next three years."

Company: "I am sorry, but $133,000 is outside our compensation range for this role."

As we've already seen, the deferred compensation creates an *immediate higher* psychological set point for their salary, but it only creates a *deferred liability* for you. All kinds of things might change at your company between now and the date they get paid, but they're not going to leave until they've secured the lump sum they know they're due. This is especially helpful if an unforeseen event occurs, even something like the sale of a company. You want to know that all of your best people are going to stay in place and keep revenues coming in.

In addition, deferred compensation makes for effective leverage in order to get the signatures you may need. In most states you are not able to demand, even if voluntarily signed, additional restrictions or commitments from an employee already in your employ if you do not have both "agreement" and "consideration." Having someone sign an agreement because they will be fired if they don't is not sufficient for enforcement. You need to have given them consideration (compensation or benefits) in return for their additional commitment. If your people haven't already signed NDAs, noncompete clauses, and other vital employee agreements, bundle them with deferred compensation to further balance your risk.

Similarly, if you haven't considered key-person insurance policies, such as life insurance policies on your key executives, that conversation goes hand in hand with deferred compensation. Many employees can get antsy at the idea of their employer "profiting" from their death. You know that all that insurance would be doing is helping you break even on the sudden loss and need to replace a key member of your team, so coupling key-person policies and deferred compensation into one conversation helps the employee see both sides of the equation.

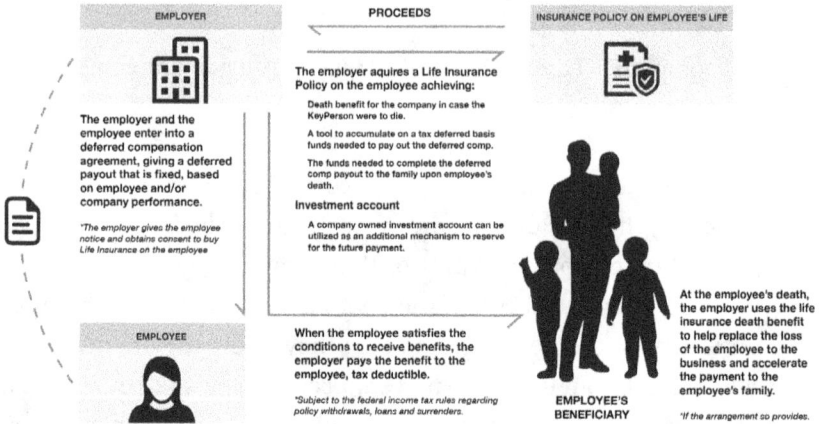

Finally, these agreements work very well in lieu of traditional bonuses. Offer them to the employees who are doing the best work and frame them as rewards for all of their efforts. You can't do the same thing with a 401(k) or defined benefit plan because, by law, you'd have to make the same modifications for all of your employees—not just the top performers. With deferred compensation, your employees will feel appreciated, and you will enjoy the benefit of knowing your business will continue profiting from their participation for at least a certain number of years.

Retirement Planning for Business Owners

Now, let's talk about how you can approach retirement planning so that it's an employer benefit and not something you view solely as a way of retaining your best people.

One of the best and simplest tools is including a Roth option in addition to the standard pre-tax program. Roth IRAs have been around since the Taxpayer Relief Act of 1997 was passed, and Roth 401(k)s have been available since 2014. We have found that most businesses don't properly utilize Roth options. In fact, the majority of the time, plan administrators don't even seem to consider them.

This big miss has negative implications for both the employees and the owner. On more than one occasion, we've met business owners who have an impressive amount of money set aside for retirement. However, they can't do in-plan conversions or Roth contributions because their administrator never set this up. That's a really big lost opportunity.

The contribution limits for IRAs and 401(k)s change from year to year, but the maximum 401(k) contribution has consistently been about three times the maximum IRA (or Roth IRA) contribution. Roth IRAs and Roth 401(k)s allow money to be deposited on an after-tax basis, with no tax on growth and no tax on future withdrawals. With our current set of tax brackets sitting on the low side of historic levels, the Roth IRA is a powerful tool for owners and employees alike to set aside money that has no vulnerability to the tax setting policy of future government administrations. Not including Roth options in a 401(k) plan limits the ability to allocate to tax-free buckets to a fraction of what they could be.

That's not the only problem. As a business owner, you have fiduciary duty to your employees where these plans are concerned. If you don't offer the best possible plans for your employees, they could hold you liable for missed opportunities of their own. Your employees could easily acquire the required documents to take you to court, too.

If you want to see just how easy this would be, send us an email at *info@ sfgway.com*. Tell us your company's legal name and the city in which you are located. With just that information, we'll acquire your company's Form 5500 and send it to you, something you may have thought was accessible only to those with a key to your filing cabinet. Your employees may not know how to find a copy, but if one of them ever speaks to a labor attorney, *they* definitely will. If that attorney finds any hint that you're limiting your employees' options or opportunities where their benefits are concerned, you could wind up in court, or worse yet, undergoing a Department of Labor audit. That's why we recommend that you hire a third party to look over the plans you offer. This person or entity will share fiduciary duties with you, shouldering a great deal of the load in case someone does actually file a lawsuit.

This third-party assessor should also document an analysis of your choices every year to make sure you are leveraging the best possible option for a 401(k). You don't want years to go by before you realize the one you had chosen was limiting how much you could set aside. As a business owner, you can put away hundreds of thousands of dollars for you and your spouse without being legally obligated to offer the exact same options to your employees. Better still, you can do this on a pre-tax basis by utilizing a defined benefit plan and stitching it together with other plans that will limit your tax exposure. Again, you'll want a third-party expert to help you with this, so you know it's done correctly.

(A word of warning on choosing your advisors—trust your retirement planning only to people who share your goals. It's not uncommon for business owners to limit their savings potential because they listen to a financial product salesperson who doesn't have their goals in mind. They're thinking about the owners' employees and what kinds of plans will work best for them.)

Another mistake owners often make is thinking that saving their money before taxes always makes the most sense. We know a very successful entrepreneur who thought this. After his third business was launched, he had a phenomenal balance sheet, but he was actually paying more in taxes than he had saved in taxes when he put the money in. We call this reverse tax planning, or paying more to the IRS over your lifetime than you need to.

While tax-deferred options can be great, you don't want to assume that's the case every single time. Carry out a lifetime assessment to see in what circumstances that would be the case.

Potential Strategies to Talk Through with Your Current Advisory Team

Going through every single investment and tax strategy you could consider is beyond the scope of this book. We would be doing you a disservice if we tried to summarize them and tell you that was sufficient information to start making decisions.

Instead, here is a list of some of the best—yet most overlooked—strategies, which you can use as a prompt to launch a discussion with your current advisory team:

(Note: if you do not currently have an advisory team . . . you should. Send an email to *info@sfgway.com* with "Build a Team" in the subject line, and our team will teach you how to start this process.)

- **Setting Aside Money Through a Backdoor Roth IRA:** You may think you make too much to benefit from a Roth IRA, but that's not necessarily the case. As long as your balance sheet is set up correctly, you can still put money away using a backdoor Roth IRA, even if you make substantially more than the $192,000 threshold usually allows.

- **Don't Pay Your Spouse Just Because:** Are you currently paying your spouse a paycheck? Did a CPA tell you to do so because otherwise, they wouldn't be eligible for Social Security? Did they say your spouse needed an income to contribute to your company's 401(k) plan? While they could be right, far too often, this approach means you're actually losing money because of payroll taxes. You'd owe less—and keep more—between the two of you if you simply added the amount you'd otherwise pay them to your own income.

- **Augusta Rule:** This is the ability to rent your own home to your business for business use for up to 14 days a year. This is tax deductible to the business and tax free to your personal balance sheet.

- **Recharacterizing Income**: If you currently have a business that does not qualify for the new 199A of the Trump Tax Plan, you may be able to recharacterize your income by separating the type. For example: You have a consulting company that does not qualify for 199A, and you make $500,000 a year, though you create all your own branding and media. Perhaps you can start an additional company that can own all of your IPs, and your primary company can pay your media company for licensing, saving as much as 20% in taxes for the profit you can shift to the media company.

- **Qualified Sick Pay Plans:** Document your company's willingness to pay owners and executives for a certain amount of time after an accident that keeps them from work (for example, something that leaves them disabled). If they're not working, you can't legally pay them and deduct the amount from your taxes. A qualified sick pay plan gives you the ability to do so for a specific period of time.
- **Owning Insurance Through a 401(k) Plan:** If structured properly, the ownership of your company can own business and personal life insurance through a 401(k). This should only be attempted after the proper analysis is done by an expert in this specialized area, and the final exit plan should be crystal clear before going in.
- **Intentionally Defective Grantor Trust (IDGT):** An IDGT can be used to transfer shares of a business to the next generation without giving up any real control over the business. This is a phenomenal option for any business owner who will eventually leave their company to their kids.
- **Holding an Internal Family Sale:** You can transfer fractional shares over time to your family members. Gifting or note sales are allowed under current tax laws at discounted rates because the recipient holds only a minority interest.
- **Cost Segregation Analysis:** This process allows you to identify personal assets that are combined with real property assets, so you can separate out the types of property and assets for tax purposes. For example, when you look at your commercial building, most costs are going to depreciate over 27.5 or 39 years. A cost segregation analysis will identify costs that could be depreciated in as few as five. As a result, you can see positive cash flow from real estate show up on your balance sheet tax free in much less time.
- **Donor-Advised Fund:** A business or an individual can use one of these funds to augment their charitable giving. It acts like a little family foundation that you can put money into in the current tax year and then give away in the future. If you have a big earnings year, a donor-advised fund allows you to defer taxes on them until

later. Said differently, it allows you to separate the deduction of the charitable giving from the making of the actual gift.

- **The Wait and See Irrevocable Life Insurance Trust (ILIT):** All too often, insurance agents and attorneys tell people to give away their life insurance to get it outside of their estate immediately. Through the proper use of gifting assets that appreciate faster than life insurance, you can get those outside the taxable estate, with the option to trade them for life insurance later.

We've covered a lot of ground in this chapter, including some of the most important decisions you have to make in order to prepare for your retirement and help your employees do the same—while keeping them on board.

Hopefully, we've helped you see why the conventional approach to planning for retirement doesn't work for people who own their own businesses. Fortunately, we're not without a number of different options. It's just about taking the time to consider them and then making the right decisions.

In the next chapter, we're going to talk about another very important financial decision, although it's one that the vast majority of people never actually make.

Chapter 9:
The Biggest Financial Decision
Most People Leave Unmade

I N THIS CHAPTER WE ARE GOING TO TALK ABOUT LIFE INSURANCE, BUT IN A different way than you are probably thinking. We will look at how life insurance pertains to the life of a business.

There are two reasons life insurance deserves its own chapter. The first is that there is a high level of general understanding around life insurance in our culture, but a low level of detailed understanding. If you held an impromptu survey, likely 90% or more of the entrepreneurs and extremely successful business owners in your life would affirm that they know exactly what life insurance does. However, they probably won't be able to actually explain how it works in detail.

Second, by explaining the applications of this tool called life insurance from the perspective of a business owner, we are looking to help you create a new method to view other financial tools differently as well. Therefore, even if you're part of the 10% who understands everything about life insurance, this chapter is still designed to have far-reaching effects on other areas of your balance sheet.

The Two Main Types of Life Insurance

Many people are surprised to learn just how many different types of life insurance there are. For the purposes of this chapter, we're just going to focus on the two main categories:

First, **term life insurance**.

As the name suggests, this type of insurance is coverage that lasts only for a certain term or amount of time. Once the term expires, you are no longer covered.

The financial industry leaves us with the impression that we can always buy another policy for another term, but there are two real issues there:

1. As we get older, new insurance costs more, so at some point, it becomes prohibitively expensive to start a new term policy.
2. There is no guarantee that you will continue to qualify for insurance from a health perspective. Even if you have the overall good health to re-qualify, do you think it is likely that you will have *exactly as good* of a bill of health 10 to 20 years down the road as you do now? Additional notes on your doctor's records over the next 10 years can be another multiplier of insurance costs down the road.

While term life insurance doesn't require a lot of cash flow and is definitely the more affordable of the two types we're covering, it will eventually become expensive enough that it no longer makes sense to pay for it.

Terms for this type of coverage can last for 1, 5, 10, 15, 20, or 30 years. For this entire time, the premium is guaranteed for the length of the term, but the policy may not be renewable when the term is up.

Once the first term is over, the cost will either go up by 10 times or it will be impossible to qualify for a new one.

For example, if you take out a policy with a 30-year term when you are 35, no insurance company will want to give you a second 30-year policy once the first one expires. The likelihood of you passing before the next one expires is just too high.

You'll also tend to have a harder time qualifying as you get older, because the insurance companies will have more years of health history to review, which usually means more reasons to decline you based on your health.

This brings us to one of the major misunderstandings of the details around life insurance. Most people think you buy life insurance with your money. You don't. You *fund* it with your money, but you buy life insurance with your health. One note from your doctor in your medical record about

TERM INSURANCE

MONEY

Increase forces cancellation

Guaranteed level period

AGE

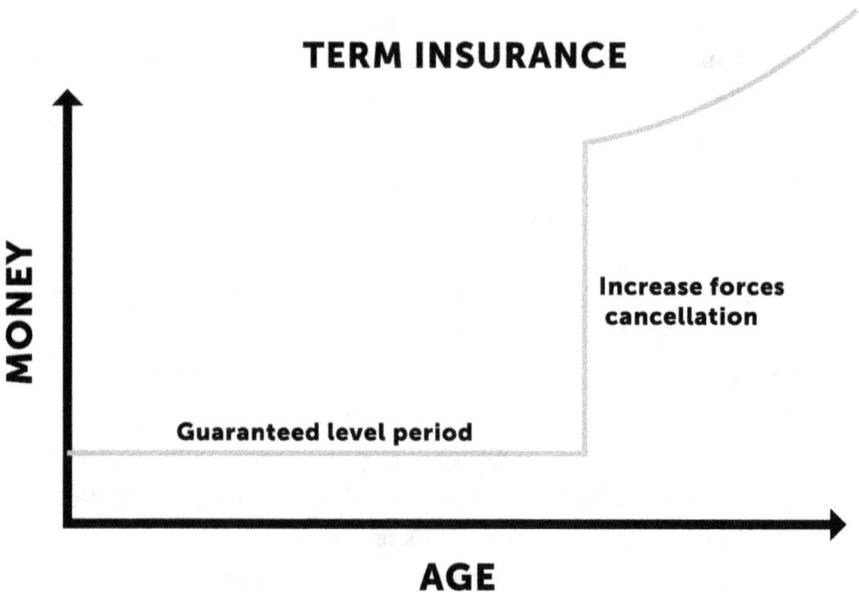

a funny-looking mole and you could find that no life insurance company is willing to offer you a policy.

By the way, it's a little-known fact that health privacy laws such as HIPAA do not protect your medical records from these insurance companies when you apply for a policy. That's because part of the application process is signing away this protection so they can review your history. If you don't allow them to do so, you won't be considered.

Life insurance companies will be extremely thorough in their research. The Medical Information Bureau (MIB) is a corporation owned by roughly 430 US insurance companies. When life insurance agencies are considering policies, they're given access to this database, so they can check every prescription and medical record available.

The second main category of life insurance is called **whole life**, and it works very differently than term insurance. The easiest way to understand whole life insurance as it is today is to start by understanding how it worked before 1982.

Back then, you could put as much money as you wanted into a whole life insurance policy. Literally, you could take a million dollars out of your savings account and deposit it into one of these policies. If there was any health history review, it was not as extensive as what we described above. This is because if you deposited that $1 million from your savings, the insurance company might give you a total life insurance policy of $1,050,000—they had very little risk over and above the money you put in.

Many smart, wealthy people were doing this, because whole life insurance offered incredible benefits. Even people who typically were drawn to the allure of higher returns in the stock market were putting a significant portion of their assets into life insurance, just because of the certainty it offered. You could reliably expect it to grow between 4% and 5% every single year. More importantly, policies were guaranteed to never go down in value. They were completely liquid, as well, and there were no state or federal income taxes on the growth. In places like New York City that have city-specific taxes, these policies were also immune from tax. On top of it all, the cash in these policies in most states was 100% creditor protected (currently in 42 states).

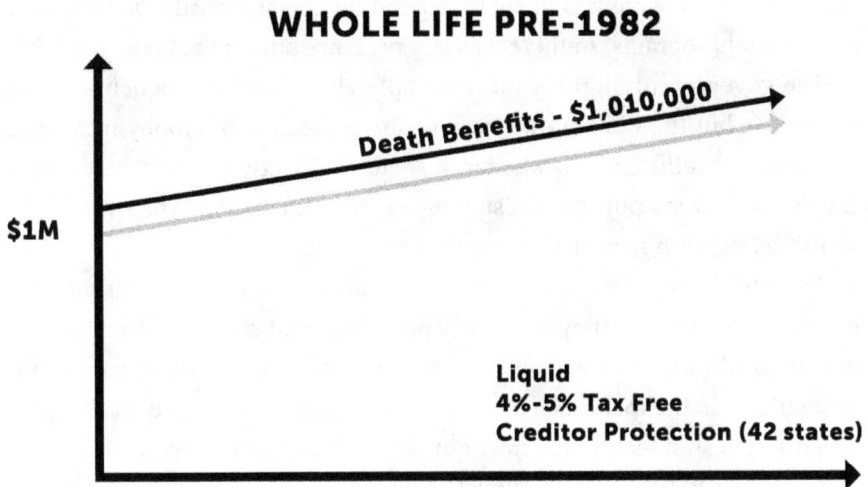

WHOLE LIFE PRE-1982

Death Benefits - $1,010,000

$1M

Liquid
4%-5% Tax Free
Creditor Protection (42 states)

Doesn't that sound amazing? If that kind of opportunity existed today, just about everyone would be rushing to put as much money as possible into it. They wouldn't even think about buying CDs, corporate CDs, corporate bonds, or municipal bonds. So, what happened?

Well, eventually, word got around that whole life insurance was an unbeliev-able opportunity that combined safety with sufficient returns. This meant Wall Street started losing significant flows of assets to the life insurance companies, and the IRS noticed they were losing a lot of tax revenue. It is hard to know for certain whether it was Wall Street lobbyists who helped the government come to realize this important fact, but you can draw your own conclusions.

Regardless of what sparked the new legislative effort, the government passed two landmark pieces of legislation between 1982 and 1988: the Tax Equity and Fiscal Responsibility Act (TEFRA) and the Technical and Miscellaneous Revenue Act (TAMRA). The most impactful change in the financial landscape was that these laws required insurance companies to take on a certain amount of risk when offering whole life types of policies.

It really was a clever bit of political maneuvering. You see, the tax bene-fits of life insurance were originally put in place because it was deemed to be a public service to encourage and incentivize families to own life insurance. If a family lost their breadwinner and had life insurance to replace that in-come, then they were less likely to depend on Social Security, welfare, and other social programs, so there was less pressure put on the taxpayer.

The government didn't want to completely remove the benefits of life insurance, but the IRS wanted to slow down the flow of money into what amounted to a lifetime tax shelter. Instead of directly limiting how much they'd let citizens put into these policies, the IRS decided they would do so indirectly with new risk requirements.

Prior to the legislation, insurance companies had very little risk. If you gave them $1 million, they were only providing that small additional death benefit. TAMRA, however, sets a limit to how much you can contribute to your whole life insurance policy. It includes an actuarial rule called the seven-pay test, which limits how quickly cash can grow inside of the con-tract relative to the amount of death benefit.

Quick question: If the IRS is limiting how much we can put into some-thing, who is it most beneficial for? (Hint: the tax-free growth of cash is probably not great for the IRS, but may be really great for you!)

After 1988, the popularity of whole life insurance took a sharp decline. It was still used by plenty of people as actual insurance, but its perceived

**WHOLE LIFE AFTER
1982 - 1987
TEFRA-TAMRA**

TEFRA-TAMRA CORRIDOR

$1M

✔ Liquid
✔ 4%-5% Tax Free
✔ Creditor Protection (42 states)

7 Years

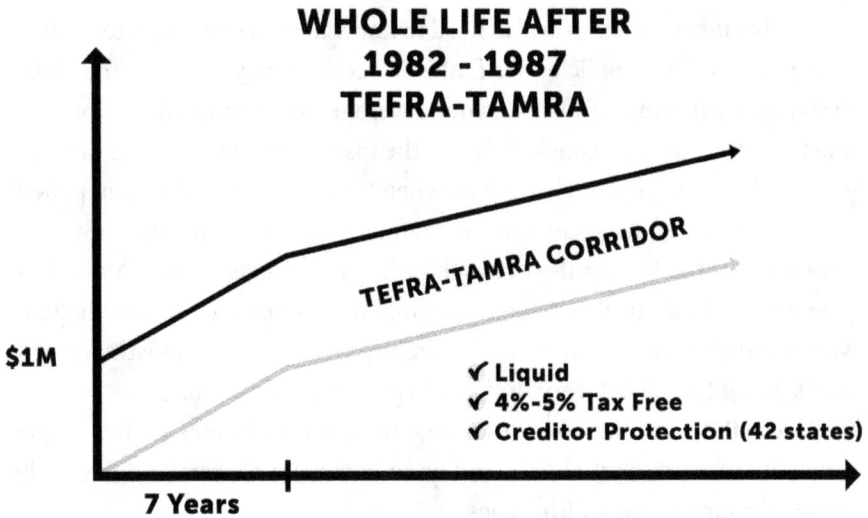

usefulness as an investment vehicle declined almost immediately for the average business owner. Meanwhile, the wealthiest of Americans and the most successful corporations and banks continue to move assets to life insurance every year, as "these policies are still great for asset allocation purposes. The only thing stopping people from taking full advantage of them is that they must be able to think more than three or four years down the road. Otherwise, it looks like a pretty poor place to put your money.

Using Life Insurance in the Business Context

Now, let's move on to how we can use these policies in a business context, in a way that will directly benefit our business, despite the laws that are in place.

As we covered in the last chapter, key-person life insurance is essential. You can take out a policy on any individual who is key to your company. That way, if they pass, you have money to help fund that key role. You also have insurance on your balance sheet to compensate your company for the loss of an important asset in that person.

Similarly, if you make an agreement with your business partner that, upon their passing, you'll buy out their spouse, one of the smartest things you can do is take out a term life insurance policy. At the very least, take it out for part of the obligation you'll owe.

As a business owner, you also need to know about convertible term insurance policies. These policies are fantastic because they give you the ability to change your mind—and, thus, your coverage—from term life to whole life. Most importantly, you can do this and the insurance company can't change your health rating from what it was when they issued you the term policy.

As an example, let's say you took out a 20-year term policy. Now, with only six months left on it—at which point, you'll need to take out a new policy—you find out you have a terminal disease or one of your hobbies would prevent you from being insurable. Obviously, in most scenarios, that's going to make it very difficult to get coverage again.

Fortunately, you have a convertible term life insurance policy, so you can switch yours to whole life and none of the details can be changed because of your recent health issues.

Structuring Life Insurance as an Asset

If you've never thought about structuring life insurance as an asset, don't be alarmed. The vast majority of people haven't. There are two very good reasons for this: the first is that most life insurance agents don't like this kind of structuring because it reduces the amount of compensation they'll end up receiving. Likewise, any other type of advisor—including a fiduciary asset manager—will end up making less if you do this, as opposed to simply letting them manage your money as they normally would. Despite what some radio host might say, the advisor charging 1.5% a year will make more money over the life of your relationship than they would with a properly structured whole life insurance policy.

That said, one of the best ways to use life insurance to improve your business's value is using what's called the still water strategy.

Picture a lake in the mountains. It has a stream that brings water into it and one that siphons it away on the other end. All that water movement tends to happen at the top, though. The closer you get to the bottom, the less you'll see the water moving around.

Most companies experience something very similar to their cash flow. If they have, say, $1 million in cash, only about $600,000 is going in and

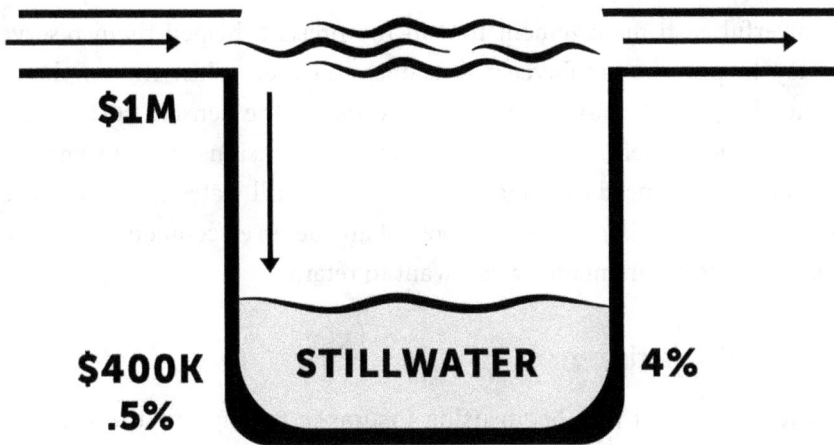

out of the company. The other $400,000 is just sitting at the bank earning maybe 0.05% in taxable interest.

If all you did was shift that money over time into a whole life insurance policy, you could be earning up to 4% in nontaxable interest and a guaranteed principal. You'd do better on a cash-on-cash basis, have just as strong of a book-value asset, and enjoy a number of other benefits including the death benefit.

Best of all, it's not costing you anything. There's no real hard cost to the policy, just the cash flow aspect and a short-term lowering of liquidity to consider.

Funding Deferred Compensation Agreements with Life Insurance

In the last chapter, we spent a lot of time talking about the value of using deferred compensation agreements to reward and retain your best employees. Another great thing about life insurance is how it can be used to fund these incredible opportunities.

The best way to do this is with key-person insurance. That way, if anything happens to the person whom you offered the deferred compensation agreement to, you have money set aside for their spouse.

Decades ago, this is very similar to how most companies provided pensions to their workers. The life insurance policies gave the company a powerful cash management tool in the present, helped them reserve money to pay the employee's pensions, and then when the employee eventually passed away, the company recouped the pension cost via the life insurance benefit. You may not be offering pensions for your employees, but the enhanced cash management of the still water strategy above may be able to similarly offset the cost of any deferred compensation plan you offer a key team member you want to retain.

Filing an EOLI Notice

Before you go out and begin using insurance to improve the value of your business, you need to know about Employer-Owned Life Insurance (EOLI) notices.

If you have owned life insurance in your company since August 17, 2006, the IRS requires that you file this notice. Part of the tax code says that life insurance bought for any business purpose may be subject to a taxable death benefit—just like income—if you don't file an EOLI notice for it.

While this may seem a bit vague, the law broadly defines employer-owned life insurance policies if any of the following happens:

- The business owner engages in any trade or business *and*
- They (or a related party) is a beneficiary (direct or indirect) *and*
- The insured party is an employee at the time the policy was issued *and*
- The insured is a US citizen or resident.

The reason behind this legislation is that corporations used to purchase what was referred to as "janitor's insurance." That's because they weren't just buying key-person insurance and taking policies out on the executives. They were taking policies out on everyone, including the janitors.

As we covered earlier, it's that valuable of an asset. It represents a guaranteed future return that's completely tax free. The only caveat is that you need someone to insure, and there's only so much of a policy you can take out on them relative to their income and age.

In the end, it was terrible optics. When the public found out that corporations were taking out insurance policies on working-class people, reactions were extremely critical. Unfortunately, the resulting legislation created a whole new set of problems for every company, even those using key-people insurance and/or implementing a key-person insurance strategy in their buy/sell agreements. Now, under 101(j) of the tax code, if you haven't filed EOLI notices for your business-owned life insurance policies, you may actually need to redo them and file proper notice and consent in order to avoid taxability. This means absent a 101(j) form filed at the time you purchased the policy, any business policy that pays out to you would be taxed at *your highest income bracket.*

Do not hesitate to reach out to us at *info@sfgway.com* if you think you have purchased life insurance since August 17, 2006, as you may have a taxable death benefit on your business balance sheet.

Buy/Sell and Covenant Agreements

It's very normal for owners to have debts on their businesses. Sometimes, this just means a simple line of credit. Most business owners have them under control, and they don't represent any real source of concern. However, that's only when everything is going as planned.

If you read your covenants on your business loan agreements, you'll almost certainly find that in the case of death, disability, divorce, or a change in ownership, the bank can call all of their notes due—meaning you need to pay them back in full immediately. How might this play out?

Say you are using life insurance to fund your buy/sell agreement. Part of said agreement is that you'll pay your business partner's spouse $1 million to buy your partner's end of the company upon their passing. That's fine, but you also have a million-dollar business loan from the bank.

Therefore, if your partner were to pass, you are obligated to give their spouse $1 million and the bank is able to call in the loan, requiring they be paid back in full before any stock can change hands. These two circumstances will stand at odds, unless you plan in advance for this kind of scenario. Make sure your buy/sell insurance planning is not *just* the amount needed to buy out a surviving spouse! If it is, you could be faced with a Sophie's choice of who you will pay, because either the bank or your deceased partner's spouse is going to sue you.

Using Life Insurance to Insure Your Company

As we said at the beginning of the chapter, most people understand the basics of life insurance—what it is and what it's meant to do. Now you know how to use life insurance for so much more than the basics.

Specifically, you've seen how life insurance can positively impact your company in a number of different ways. Hopefully, you now have a new perspective on a number of different financial matters, too. By just changing your perspective slightly, you can take full advantage of the number of options available for improving your company's value and, thus, that of your personal balance sheet.

Chapter 10:
The Financial Sales Machine That Is Chewing Up Your Finances

A s we both started early in the financial industry, we have had the chance to see several ways that financial institutions grow their distribution. Traditional stockbrokers didn't just go away; they were replaced by automated systems and consumer platforms like E*TRADE. Big-box investing houses now offer insurance, while insurance companies now have asset management divisions. Robo-advisors seek to put the whole investing experience on autopilot. Unlicensed "edutainers" write books (and make money giving advice) that tell people how to fire their financial advisor.

These various models have developed over the last 50 years, and they are all largely still in existence today. Keep in mind, nearly all of these major sources for financial advice are built fundamentally as a sales model. The entire personal financial advice industry is based on the late 1960s investment-opportunity-driven sales model (remember *Glengarry Glen Ross*?). Because of this, it's harder and harder for clients to make good decisions and acquire the best financial products that can help them care for their future monetary concerns.

Everyone is hoping that they are making good decisions with their money, though often they do not know where to look. Every day we see high-income households scan the marketplace for financial opinions and advice, and often they have no idea how to categorize the different sources they are getting information from.

As a way to ease you out of the cozy fireside chat of this book and back out into the real world, in this final chapter we will give you an outline of how to think about the different categories of financial help, along with their pros and cons.

Financial Entertainers

Financial entertainers are the folks that we read about in books, articles, blog posts, YouTube, and radio. They are mostly unlicensed individuals who have built a brand of giving specific advice with incomplete information about the person whom they are advising. This advice is designed to be given between commercials while being short, pithy, and entertaining. You will notice that when you buy one of their books at the bookstore, no one asks you what you make in income a year or anything about your personal situation. That's because everyone buying that book is getting the same advice.

What is the primary objective of a financial entertainer? To attract as many consumers to their material as possible. Why do they need so many people reading or listening to them? It's simple: their devoted listeners or readers are the product they sell to their advertisers and publishers. The advertisers are the ones who are trying to put their products and services in front of the listeners.

This leads to each of the financial entertainers targeting the "average" American. The real median average American household income is $61,372, and 90% of US households make less than $139,713. The top 5% of household income is $197,651, and the top 1% incomes start at $480,804. Financial entertainers cannot target the highest-income earners, as they would have next to no audience. Thus, the likelihood of finding good information that will apply to you as a high-income-earning entrepreneur, professional, or executive, is nearly zero.

Pro: This advice is free on the radio, the internet, and at the library, and can be good for an "aha" moment. Reading a specific passage might lead to the insight that you have been spending too much or that you need to speak differently with your spouse about money.

Con: The advice is too general and will likely not fit you and your family, especially not if you have income in the top income of US households.

Robo-Advisors

If you have not yet heard of a robo-advisor, they are the investment management firms that are run via a blend of analytical tools and call centers that focus on you getting a low-cost portfolio—as long as it is in one of the preset portfolios that they offer. Robo-advisors determine your level of risk tolerance and simply allocate your money into several categories, with the mindset that the best way they can serve clients is by managing their assets for the lowest possible cost, allowing the client to interact with a call center rather than an advisor.

Robo-advisors have great commercials and a slick user interface design for their apps and websites. All of the above is in service of their primary goal: making investing with them feel *easy*. The problems with these platforms are caused by what they do not handle: all of the things outside of the specific investment allocation and models that they are there to sell you.

With these models you can pay additionally to have someone take a more comprehensive look at what you are doing, though you do not typically get the person who can handle high-end tax planning, nontraditional investment assessment, or strategic thinking on the sale of a business or other major liquidity event.

Pro: People do not worry about being sold a product. The investment management price tag (expense ratio) is low. Robo-advisors offer a simple set of investment models and guide you into the model that their automated questionnaire suggests will be appropriate for your risk tolerance.

Con: The expense ratio is not the only source of cost in a portfolio, and all of those other sources of cost may not be managed. There is very little chance you will get custom advice or coaching. If you are a household using a robo-advisor, there is usually one financially savvy spouse utilizing the service. The spouse using the service is typically not learning more, and the less active, less savvy spouse is not learning at all. Said differently, robo-advisors give you access to investments in an area you already know and are comfortable with.

Financial Salespeople

These come in many flavors with varying titles, including the coveted CFP, CFA, RFP, ChFC, CLU, LUTCF, and so forth. This is by far the largest group of people that you are likely to run into. They are referred to you by friends and family. They meet you at a networking event. They send you a connection request on LinkedIn.

These folks mostly make their money from commissioned sales of products. They do not charge a fee in advance, though they may also offer fee-based asset management in addition to product sales.

This has become an area of confusion in the financial industry, so let's first look at the difference between commissions and fee-based asset management, as the industry defines them:

- *Commission-based financial advice* is when an advisor is getting a percentage of your initial investment by way of first-year commissions and/or renewals. This is usually a relatively higher initial percentage of the money you invest, with very low or zero future recurring commissions over time.
- *Fee-based financial advice* is when an advisor charges by the hour, an up-front fee, or a flat fee as a percentage of the assets that they manage every year. They are distinguished from the "fee-only" advisors in the next section because this group can charge investment fees, but they may also earn commissions in other areas.

While many fee-based financial advisors would like you to believe that commission-based financial advisors and fee-based financial advisors are as far from each other as the east is from the west, we would offer you a different interpretation.

Distinction Without a Difference

Both of these, commission salespeople and fee-based financial advisors, are simply in sales with different types of compensation methodologies.

The largest complaint about commission-based financial advisors is that they have an incentive to put you in high-commission products that may not be appropriate for you. The new fiduciary standard that's gotten a lot of notoriety in the last five years has called attention to the problems with merely a "suitability standard" and pushed many advisors further toward fee-based asset management, with a huge collective sigh of relief from regulators and clients alike. The wolves of Wall Street, if not turned totally into sheep, are at least being defanged and declawed by having their interest in *commission* replaced by *fee-based* compensation that safely aligns the interest of the client and the advisor.

Or so it may seem. Here is the problem that the American consumer seems to have missed: the advisor who only manages money for a flat fee each year still has their own set of inherent self-interests. In fact they have an absolute interest in being the one who manages all of your money, and in continuing to be in that seat year after year. You can ask yourself this question: Could a fee-based financial advisor also be selling you a product—one that simply compensates them 1.5% per year every year that you own it?

Many commission-based financial advisors work for larger institutions who heavily limit what products that advisor can sell their clients. For instance, if you see an insurance company's name on the outside of the office where your advisor works, chances are they are highly incentivized and/or exclusively restricted to sell only that company's products. You can quickly see how that would shape the way those advisors are originally recruited, the way that they are trained, and what they are incentivized to sell. This limited education and the corporate restrictions limit the advice they can offer their clients.

There are also times when someone holds themselves out as a fee-based financial advisor who is also a fiduciary, but depending on their practice, you might still categorize them as a financial salesperson. For instance, do they have a way to make money other than by directly managing your money?

Whether your advisor is a commission-based financial salesperson or a fee-based asset management financial salesperson, you will notice one common thread: they will consistently and predictably steer you toward driving more money under their management. If you want a unique test for your advisor, or your new potential advisor, you could simply ask them to review a real estate deal that you would like to participate in. Some of the largest financial services firms in the world have restrictions on their advisors from even being able to offer you advice in any transaction that would occur outside of the specific sets of products that they could sell you. (Note: the advisor may be willing to offer you advice in a call or in a meeting, but the test is to see if the advisor will send you their assessment in writing.)

This type of advice is often wrapped in a warm blanket of a close relationship. That close connection often clouds your judgment as you make financial decisions. It is not uncommon for our advisors to meet a client who has been very poorly served, or even taken advantage of, by someone who is their "longtime friend" or golf buddy.

While it does seem nice that someone would be willing to offer you a great deal of advice without collecting a check from you up-front, make no mistake that this is simply a part of their sales process. They want to bring enough value to you that you feel deeply obligated to transact with them to buy whatever product it is that they eventually offer you. While this is by far the most common way that financial advice is offered across the country, it would be the equivalent of you (or your health insurance) never paying your doctor for their time, and instead your doctor made 100% of their money based upon the prescriptions or tests they prescribed to you.

This doesn't have to produce bad results. We personally know dozens and dozens of highly ethical professionals using this model. The key is to make sure they use a consistent set of financial calculators with you, that help both of you understand and double-check the math that backs up their recommendations.

Pro: This type of financial sales is readily accessible to most all of America. Because there is no up-front fee to meet with them, you can receive proposals from several advisors and bounce their philosophies off of one another. For middle- to low-income families, this may be the most cost-efficient way to receive help from a live human professional, who has received at least a modicum of training.

Con: This system can seem economical up-front. The long-term problem is the amount of time that it takes to double-check the advisor (and yourself). This model requires you to go out into the marketplace on a regular basis and have conversations with other advisors to be sure you have gotten the greatest advice. Unfortunately, you end up in the unenviable position of interacting with additional advisors in this model, who are also vying for your business by working for free while trying to court you.

Fee-Only Financial Advisors (or Fiduciaries)

A fee-only financial advisor is a rare bird, and for good reason. The basic principle here is that they only make money when they are paid directly by you, the client. They do not accept any form of compensation from outside parties.

Inside of the fee-only financial advisor population, there is a group that charges only an annual retainer or by the hour. The other camp may offer those types of fee structures, but they will also use fees that are based on a percentage of the assets they manage for you.

Both of these groups refer to themselves as fiduciaries. While the legal structure they operate under dictates that they put their clients' interest first above all others, we maintain that for practical purposes this "clients' interest first" standard may not always be followed. When they say they put your interest first, it means that they fully disclose their compensation as well as take the same compensation on each of their client portfolios, so that at least their gross revenue is not impacted by the recommendations they make to you. So under the law they can clearly show that they took no *active* step that would put their interests above yours, and that gets all the attention.

What we should be concerned about is what they do not advise us on, or what forms of *inaction* might in fact be under-supporting your interests.

One of the ways you can check is to ask these questions:

- What do you recommend if we find that as a result of my planning I require life insurance? Does your team handle or facilitate that?
- What do you do when you find that your clients require disability insurance?

- If you refer this work out to others, what percent of your clients execute on the recommendations that you make on life and disability insurance?

Over the years of recruiting and coaching financial advisors, we have seen many situations where the "fiduciary advisor" (sometimes said with a touch of snootiness) is asked if they handle disability insurance. They simply reply with a lament on how difficult the underwriting is, how it is tough for them or their staff, or how it risks upsetting their clients. This is how you know they are selling. Have you ever had a doctor back off of recommending a difficult treatment that could save a person's life because it is inconvenient for them or could upset their patient? That is the opposite of professionalism.

Only the rarest of these fiduciary birds actually do the hard work needed to be sure that the client is covered in all areas of their finances. The rest merely claim the title but hardly pay attention. You may then be wondering why the latter portion would even claim to be fiduciary advisors and charge a flat fee rather than earn commission. What they're attempting to do in their outward-facing compensation methodology is to throw off anyone from thinking that they are biased as it relates to their planning. They cannot escape the truth that we've come to understand, though. Everyone is biased.

For proof, consider the following example of two financial advisors. One advisor grew up in a household where her father was incredibly successful in real estate and was able to send her and her siblings to a highly rated university, where she got her degree in business. Her parents are retired now and have enough financial independence to spend plenty of time with her family and her children.

The second financial advisor's father did not do so well in real estate. After initially building a seven-figure net worth in real estate, his father fell on hard times. A combination of tax law changes and interest rate hikes made his entire real estate portfolio turn upside down. This change in fortune caused the advisor's parents to divorce, which then led his father to make some horrible lifestyle choices. This financial advisor had to work part-time jobs and took on a great deal of student loans as he struggled to put himself through school, all the while doing his best to help his younger siblings deal with the divorce and the subsequent infighting between their parents.

If you were to ask these two advisors what their opinion is on real estate investing, even though you paid an hourly fee for their advice, you are not going to get an independent or unbiased answer. We all look at the world through a veil of our specific biases. The act of paying fees for the advice does not alone avoid biases.

We mentioned that some fee-only financial advisors take only hourly fee product work, the classic "billable hours" model. While this does seem like the most pure model, we have some simple math for you to consider. A 40-hour workweek will almost never generate 40 billable hours, and out of 52 weeks there are hopefully at least a few vacation weeks built in. Therefore, let's assume that they can actually produce 20 billable hours per week on average. Then we need to subtract their rent and staff costs, the cost of any software they use for their planning, and any marketing budget. Obviously the billable hours model has produced success for other professionals, like attorneys and consultants. But we have only rarely seen financial advisors in an hourly-fee model who are willing and able to charge the same kind of hourly rates that consumers have come to expect from big law firms or consultants.

What you find is a business model that rarely has the ability to allow that advisor to be in the top 1% of household income earners. We don't take issue with the fact that some advisors might make less money in this model. It isn't even the fact that an advisor might not earn an above-average income that presents a problem. The issue is that this hourly model virtually *guarantees* that the advisor will have an artificially limited set of income outcomes. It begs the question: Do you want to take financial advice from somebody whose own freely chosen business model comes with an artificially low ceiling on their earning potential?

Pro: You get the advice that is based upon the advisor's opinion and experience. You can understand the cost of your advice up-front, either due to the hourly rate or the flat fee that the advisor charges to retain them every year.

Con: Even though they share with you that they are a fiduciary, you do not get let off the hook for your own responsibility. You must have a system of checks and balances in your planning that would allow for you to assess the advice of even the fee-only financial advisor.

A New Model: Wealth Design/Build

As you can see, none of these models allow a client to have transparency in the planning process, or give the client enough education to make their own decisions. Every model listed above gives limited information while asking the client to make their decisions based upon the advisor's implied authority (lettered credentials after their name), their salesmanship, or the relationship.

The American public deserves better. Think for a moment about how you compensate every other professional (CPA, attorney, outsourced CFO, and so on) in your life. You either pay them hourly for the work that they do, or you pay them a flat fee or retainer to help you with a project or set of projects.

The architecture industry, for example, is much older than the sales-driven financial industry, and architects have for many years charged a flat project fee to their clients to design buildings that they want. It is nearly always a simple, straightforward, and yet in-depth transaction. You start by giving the architect an idea of your resources (land, capital, budget, and timeline) and your vision for the project. The architect then helps you understand whether or not those resources are enough to create the future you desire. Next, the architect educates you on some of the basics of building codes and physical/structural limitations that could prevent or enable the future that you're after. After much discussion and revisiting of several drafts, you and the architect create a design plan for your perfect home. You are then free to take that design out into the world to make it real.

The next step is choosing a general contractor to build your home. You might have a longtime friend that you have known since high school whom you would like to be your general contractor, or you might ask around for a recommendation. You might even choose to take on the project yourself. Finally, if your architect operates a **design/build** firm, you could walk those plans from the architect's office, down the hall, and hand them to the in-house general contractor.

When you deal with a salesperson, the first thing that you ask is: What is the price? An architect, by contrast, would never start by giving you a price for them to design a home for you. That is because working with each set of resources is unique. Sure, the architect might volunteer a general fee range that they tend to operate in, so that you both know neither of you is wasting each other's time. But you would never even consider asking an architect for a final quote in your first meeting, and if you did, they wouldn't be able to answer the question.

To apply the discourse of architecture to your planning, we have taken a different approach from the rest of the financial industry. First, you want to be sure that you have a philosophical alignment with the advisor and the team that are going to help quarterback your financial decisions. That philosophy should remain the same regardless of a client's network, personal circumstances, or lifestyle choices.

Every architect has a portfolio of work, which communicates their philosophy of building and their capacity as a professional. While a financial advisor cannot show you the work that they've done for other clients, because that work is confidential, they can openly and regularly communicate their philosophy to their clients and to the interested public.

Whenever you consider working with a financial advising firm, you should start by understanding their philosophy. We are not referring to the philosophy that they share in their sales meetings, but the philosophy that we can find demonstrated in their articles, videos, books, and public speaking engagements. This book is an example of our philosophy demonstrated. You can find more about our firm by looking online at our other articles, the resources we made available as a result of this book, and our ongoing podcast and video clips on YouTube. If someone feels they have philosophical alignment with us, we begin with a conversation about your financial philosophy and future. In that first conversation we will help you look at the future that you want to create, have a discussion about the values that you and your family have that fuel the purpose behind that future, and begin to identify the resources it will take for you to arrive there.

After that initial conversation we will give you a chance to apply to become a client of our firm. That will allow us to have an ethical discussion about whether it is appropriate for us to work together. It really is a matter of ethics, because we do not want to make an offer to work with anyone unless we are confident we can bring real value in the first year of our relationship.

For many clients, this is likely a new way to engage a financial advisor. With that in mind, we have worked with the financial regulatory authorities to make the choice as low risk as possible for new clients. If we make you an offer to work together, we include an option for a total refund of your initial engagement fee within the first six months, for any subjective reason. If you feel like you didn't receive what you thought you would, tell our team, and they will send you a check.

Through our initial process, we have a series of meetings in which our team walks side by side with you to help you begin the series of financial actions that will help fulfill that future that you sketched out during our first meeting. As you complete each meeting, we make sure that you understand and are comfortable with each decision that you make before implementation. All meetings are completed via an online meeting room that allows us all to share audio, video, and screens, so that we can support you where you are without the scheduling challenges and time commitment of driving back and forth to a big-box financial retailer's office.

As implementation of financial strategies begin, we give you the option to build your plans yourself, engage an outside party, or have our team help you build the financial structures we are recommending. Through that process we will look at the whole of your financial affairs to help you align all of your past and future financial decisions with the future that you want to create.

First we look at your current protection to put safeguards in place, so that the hard work you have already done building your income and balance sheet are protected.

- Car insurance
- Homeowners insurance
- Umbrella insurance
- Business liability protections
- Wills and trusts
- Ownership of assets

- Long-term care planning
- Business agreements
- Disability insurance
- Life insurance

We then look at household cash flow to be sure you are being efficient and effective with the money that you take out of your business. We also help you begin using a Wealth Coordination Account as the centerpiece of your financial strategies.

Then we move on to investment strategy. Here we utilize a Nobel Prize–winning asset management philosophy that we call the Sound Financial Group Passive Structured Investment Theory. During this stage, we look at the collection of investments that you have now and begin to assess that portfolio for any efficiencies that could be gained by making adjustments in line with an academically allocated and globally diversified portfolio.

This initial design phase will require an investment on your part to engage in 5 to 6 planning sessions over 8 to 10 weeks. At the end of that process, we update your One-Page Strategic Plan, which will help you navigate each 90-day period for the remaining year, helping both our team and your household make financial decisions that are in alignment with the future that you want to create.

Which Approach Is Right for You?

If you began reading this book with what you feel like is a good relationship with a financial advisor, here is a five-question litmus test you can give yourself about your current advisor relationship:

1. Did they share their philosophy with you *before* they dug into your specific financial situation?
2. If they did share their philosophy with you, can you verify it in a publicly available body of work, such as interviews, published articles, books, or at the very least, their website and marketing materials?
3. After you had a chance to sample their philosophy and business model, did they first assess your financial position (not only your

assets but also the complexity of your business) and your level of financial knowledge before telling you what it would cost to complete their process?

4. Did they give you an option to have them be your designer and allow someone else to build the plan that they designed?

5. Would you introduce this advisor to those you care about?

6. If you found that you answered any of the above with a no or "unsure," then you may be working with someone who is not a financial architect, nor a financial coach, but simply a financial salesperson with the title "advisor" on their business card. That kind of revelation isn't by itself a reason to change your relationship, but we would encourage you to refer back to earlier in this chapter, and examine the additional work you will need to do to make sure you are receiving the best results from that relationship.

To begin changing this industry, we simply put out our unique philosophy and encourage other advisors to embrace it. But for the industry to change, it will require that the very customers on whom the advisors depend push back on them. We encourage you to not let this book be a colorful decoration on your shelf, a paperweight, or a doorstop. Use the concepts and conversations we've started in this book as a catalyst for change in your financial life.

Give this book to all the players on your current financial team. If you do not have that team, then it may be a sign that engaging a firm like ours could be the first step in ensuring that your business becomes the mechanism by which you build your wealth and thereby create the financial independence and autonomy you wanted when you first started your business.

Always looking forward to our next, or our first conversation,

Paul Adams

Cory Shepherd

For Additional References, Articles, and Resources visit _YBYWbook.com_!

www.ingramcontent.com/pod-product-compliance
Lightning Source LLC
Chambersburg PA
CBHW050642190326
41458CB00008B/2389